Tidbits of Insight
for Creating Optimism

Jolly Doodle Edition

Other books by K.DeLaughter:

500 Tidbits of Insight: Living with and Overcoming Depression

Tidbits of Insight for Creating Optimism

ISBN: 0692257829
ISBN 13: 978-0692257821

To my family and friends

Table of Contents

I

<u>Creating a Realistic Mindset</u>

The best place to start making life changes is inside your mind. Your thoughts are powerful. While it is possible to obsess too much about thinking positively, there is a great deal of good that can come from being more aware of your thoughts and choosing thoughts that cultivate goodness.

In this section, you will find useful pieces of advice and ideas about creating a healthy attitude within yourself. Some ideas found in this chapter are very traditional while others are less so, but any or all of these ideas may help you build the kind of inner peace you need so that you can achieve the kind of life you want to experience. There are also several drawings and doodles to provide visual entertainment and enjoyment as you read.

This selection of tidbits are not a cure all for your ailments, nor the solution to every problem, but as a collection, they may provide you with different perspectives about how to think about the world around you, your place within it, and how to transform your uniqueness into the kind of peaceful, happy bliss you truly deserve.

◇◇◇◇◇◇◇◇

It is okay to not have all the answers. It is unrealistic to expect that you will always know what to do next. As a human, you are going to have times in your life when you just simply do not know something. It is okay.

Right now, you are a different person than you were. You have changed already. You will continue to change more. The person you will become in the future will be different from who you are now or ever were in the past. You are many different people in one lifetime. Use the knowledge that you have acquired in your past to work towards building a better you and life. May the person you are creating through all your hard work, the future you, be wiser for it.

Different people experience the same events differently. Try your best not to assume that there is a universal right way to react to a problem. You need to respond to your situation the way that you need to and not in the exact same manner your parents, friends, or neighbors. Sometimes, you may react similarly, but most of the time, you need to be simply your true, authentic self.

Making a list of goals is good, but reinventing the way you define accomplishment is better. As you change, your goals will also change. Make sure to from an opinion about what you consider to be an accomplishment. You get to define what accomplishment looks like and feels like. Refrain from just adopting a definition from family, friends, or others in your life. Define success in a way that is meaningful to you and brings you joy and fulfillment.

You are more than a single event or decision. Avoid giving yourself labels based on a single mistake or a one-time shortcoming. Self-imposed negative labels originating out of these single instances may create further stress and anxiety. You are far too valuable to shortchange yourself with such labels.

You have time. Your life path can and will wait while you help yourself. Sometimes, you will deal with a great hardship. Some times in life are cumbersome and arduous. This is a big deal and deserves to be respected as such. You are likely still able to do all of your big life plans and dreams. You will have the time, but right now, today, just focus on you. Focus on working towards a healthier future for you.

You deserve to be loved. You can choose to love yourself. There is no need to wait. You are capable of treating yourself with compassion, kindness, and admiration. You do not need permission or approval from anyone to start showing yourself the kindheartedness you deserve.

The situation you are in is temporary. You may feel a desire to panic. Do not let this happen. The pain and suffering you are currently feeling will go away. It might take time, but it will pass. There is a day in your future when you will not be suffering. There is a day in your future when you will feel happy.

You might have to invent or create what you need. The world has not failed you, nor have you failed yourself. It just may be the case that you know what you need in order to achieve a healthier life and no one else has made it yet. Go ahead and get started designing and contriving. Make the tools and resources you need. You deserve to pursue your goals.

Avoid creating excuses for good things that happen. Not every good thing that goes your way is mere coincidence. Try resisting the temptation to diminish its goodness. You deserve to have good things happen in your life. You may have earned the positive outcome, or perhaps it happened because of hard work or good planning. Try to enjoy it.

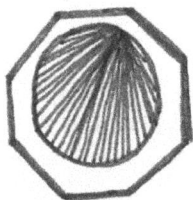

You are more than a body. Your physical appearance and existence is just a part of who you are. You have many other aspects that identify you. Your value cannot be captured in a single photograph, or weighed on a simple scale. You are more than a number, more than a size, more than an oxygen-consuming being, and more than you may have ever realized. Accept the great depth of your identity and embrace all of your qualities.

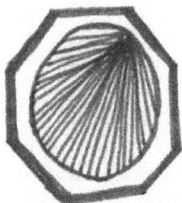

Make the best decision you can with the information you have. You might not have all the information you want before you need to make a decision. Just focus on doing your best today. It is okay if your choice is not fantastic. Occasionally, a fantastic option is not available and the best choice is simply less bad than alternatives. It happens. You have not failed at anything—just make the most of your situation.

Give yourself permission to be sad sometimes. The human body is not designed to be happy all of the time.

There are going to be spells when you feel horrible. Having a day filled with negative moods does not mean that you are mentally or emotionally unstable. It may mean that you are just having natural, logical negative reactions to events in your life that are worthy of such acknowledgement. Give yourself permission to be upset about things that you need to be upset about and allow yourself to be you.

You can always control your attitude. You can always choose how you are going to evaluate anything you observe or experience. Not all emotions or thoughts are within your control, but the opinions you have often are. You can choose to hope for a positive experience while waiting for it to occur or anticipating its outcome. No one and no situation can take this choice from you.

Instead of asking what is normal, begin to ask what is normal *for you.* A popular movie or song may spark a type of emotional reaction in the people around you, but not you. This is okay. Part of the human experience is accepting your unique self. Try your best not to obsess about being similar to other people. Whatever you are feeling is exactly what you should be feeling.

You can do something about your situation. No matter where you, or are or how you feel, there is always something you can do. Sometimes the best thing to do is just to get up and leave. It is okay to feel overwhelmed sometimes. It is also okay to react by doing what you need to do, even if it is as simple and effective as removing yourself from a situation. It happens to everyone from time to time.

You are not damaged. You are not a person of lesser value because of your circumstances or your situation. You are no less important no matter what happens to you. Things will happen that are outside of your control, but none of them influences your worth. You are still a human being of full value.

Life is not fair, but that is not your problem to fix. The more you obsess about how unfair your current life situation may be, the more it will hold you back from creating the future you want to live. The more you attempt to make life fairer for others, the less energy you have to help yourself get to the place where you need to be. Try your best to not take it all personally, and move forward towards a better future free of resentment.

You can only give one hundred percent. Once you have maxed out your attention and energy, then that is it. There does reach a point where you are doing everything that you can. When living these moments, validate your hard work and your effort. Tell yourself that you truly are giving it your all and do not be too hard on yourself.

It is not a competition. You may encounter people who have an expectation of you, or you may even have an expectation of yourself, that you will achieve a milestone within an invented time frame or specific date. Ignore all of that. You are not racing against someone else's clock to get to where you need to go. You have not done anything wrong if you do not reach a goal by this invented, and often arbitrary, due date. Take the time you need, reassess the goals that you set for yourself, and stop competing with others.

Let go of the idea of a perfect person. There is no such thing as being perfect. Try not to aim for perfection, or even perfect actions. Instead, aim for being the healthiest you in your power to create. Aspire to practice healthy habits that increase your overall happiness.

Forgive yourself. You have the power to forgive yourself for anything and everything. Your forgiveness of yourself is just as strong, if not more important, than your forgiveness of others or of others' forgiveness of you. You can decide to discontinue the blame, the disappointment, and the resentment that you may be holding on to for unbeneficial reasons. It is not serving you, so let it go.

Replace it with different thoughts, opinions, and feelings that are positive.

However long it takes you to travel on your current journey is how long it should take. Try your best not to buy into any hype that there is only one way to travel towards your goals. Accept and love your unique journey to your future and allow yourself all the time you need to get there. You deserve to enjoy the trip, and not be rushed past meaningful experiences.

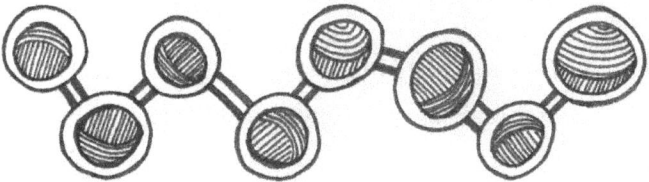

Your awareness is a gift. Be selective on who and what you choose to focus your attention. Also, be choosy about which events or experiences you take part in and enjoy. You attention is very meaningful and powerful. It is how you can show love and compassion. It is a way you can communicate what ideas you feel are worthy of your time and interest.

You are not a flawed and defective person. What is happening to you right now, the situation you are in, is not your whole identity. Your experiences may be unfortunate. Situations may be unfavorable. Plans of actions that you design may have flaws. An object you own may have parts that are defective, but not you. You are a person with an identity that is unique and special. Your value is not flawed or defective. Keep your identity and value out of the mix when you pinpoint areas of your life you wish to improve.

Feeling bad is only that, nothing more. Try not to assume that feeling bad means that you are a bad person, life is bad, or that reality is bad. Your feelings exist and fluctuate independently, so respect them as such.

You do not have to apologize for how you feel. Whether you are happy or sad, it does not matter. You do not need to feel any amount of shame for your emotions or say you are sorry for having them. You are you and if right now you are feeling an extreme mood, then so be it. Embrace and accept yourself by not apologizing when your feelings make you or someone else feel uncomfortable.

You do not have to have an opinion. You may spend days and weeks learning about something only to be just as indifferent as when you started. That is okay. You do not have to have a strong opinion about everything. It might seem like everyone you know likes or loves something, but you do not. This is fine. It does not mean you do not care, it just means you do not have a favorite or a side you favor. Part of the being human is accepting that you do not have the time or energy to form an opinion about literally everything you encounter. There is nothing wrong with this.

You are not the only one. Hardships are not new. Tough life choices are not new. Difficult situations are also not new. You are not the first person to develop a problem, an obstacle, or simply yearn for a better life. There are those who did not overcome their problems, and there are many who have. This means that there are people you can ask for guidance and useful advice. If your family and friends are unable to help you, you have people you can turn to. There are many stories of all different types of journeys, and many opportunities to connect with others. You are not alone in your desire to live a more positive life and obtain more happiness.

Embrace and love you as you are. There is no need to wait until the future to accept the entire you. You can practice random thoughts of kindness towards yourself in the present moment. Accept yourself as you are, let go of any expectations that only if you were different in some way would you be worthy of such positive praise. You deserve to be loved by you. Take a break from any negative self-talk you may be experiencing and give yourself some admiration.

You can choose to be optimistic. You can always make the conscious choice to be hopeful, rather than assume that your immediate future is awful. Optimism is something you can practice every day, even with your most private thoughts.

There is an existence beyond you. Some may call this a higher power, but you may call it whatever you wish. Having an understanding that there is some type of entity beyond you will probably help you move forward in a more positive direction. Accepting that you are not the center of it all helps to put yourself into a healthier, more grounded viewpoint of reality. You are part of a greater whole of some sort. Its name, the exact nature of your relationship with it is all up to you to discover and realize. Finding peace with your beliefs regarding your relationship with life outside of your existence is something you have the power to do.

You do not need to prove someone wrong in order to be happy, successful, or healthy. Your self-worth and overall state of mind is not contingent on a series of events that demonstrate or show someone how valuable you are. There is no life requirement that states you must prove your boss, teacher, parent, or friend wrong before moving forward in your life. You can move forward and onwards whenever you wish. You can work towards being happy, successful, and healthy without being spiteful.

Occasionally, you may be the only one who understands you. That really is okay. It might be difficult to allow your own self-credit and praise to be enough. However, your rationale may be the only one you can obtain or understand right now. There are times in everyone's life when no one else really gets it. You may be the only one that truly understands what you are experiencing at the depth you desire. It is fine. You are not as weird as you might think. It is okay to yearn for more connections with other people, but assure yourself that it is truly okay if right now, you are providing all the validation that you truly need. It happens sometimes and you have the power to provide yourself with this kind of support and love.

Your experiences are always real. The human body is not an accurate recording device. Our memories are not extremely accurate or reliable down to the last detail. However, this does not mean that what you are experiencing is somehow not a part of reality or is not really happening. It just means that you may perceive or react to your surroundings differently than before, or even differently than how others may react to an environment. Big life events, especially ones that cause great change, can do this. It is okay. If your reaction is also different from how other people react to the same events, that too is okay. What you are experiencing is still part of reality and your reactions are undoubtedly very real. Take the time and energy to accept your authentic reactions to your unique life experiences.

Remove the word hate from your vocabulary. Try using the word 'dislike' instead. Have a go at using phrases like 'that did not appeal to me' or 'I do not enjoy that'. Even when you think, try to use a different word other than 'hate'. Removing that word from your daily vocabulary will start the process of seeing the world in the many shades of gray and colors that it is.

You deserve to live your life well. You are of equal worth on some basic level to all other people on the planet. You have an equal right to live and to pursue a healthy life that you enjoy. Refrain from listening to any viewpoint, even if it is your own, telling you otherwise.

How you react to the events of your life is important.
You cannot control all aspects of yourself or all the things that will happen to you. What most often is within your control is how you choose to respond. You are capable of choosing to respond in a healthy manner. You have the strength to select behavior that supports you and does not bring you down. This is always your choice.

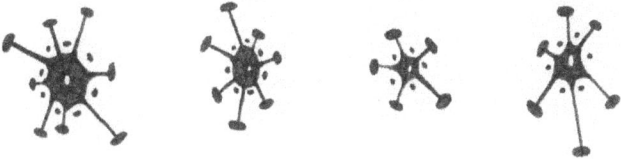

Sometimes, all you need is faith in yourself.
There are times when you might not have every single resource that you want in your possession before you act on an opportunity. Go ahead and take action anyway. Just by placing a bit of faith in your ability to capitalize on a good situation, you may find that you can do a lot more than you originally realized.

You have the right to decide what is meaningful to you.
It is a big responsibility, but it is you who will choose the story of your life. You can choose how you are going to react and respond to the events you experience. It is your decision if you want to hold grudges or forgive. It is your choice whether you wish to be angry or to let it go. If you

are dissatisfied with how an important event sits with you, then choose to make it less important. If something that others say is not a big deal, really is a big deal to you then it is okay to admit that.

Strive to do better today than you did yesterday. Long term planning may seem overwhelming. Problems that span days and weeks may add lots of stress to your life. Focus on and care more about how you are doing today compared to yesterday. You have the power to do small things right now that will help make today a better day.

Give yourself rewards for effort. Focusing on progress and accomplishments is exciting, but remember to give yourself credit and rewards for all of your efforts. The fact that you are dedicating a lot of your time and energy to working on improving your life is always worthy of your praise.

You might need to react emotionally to something more than once. It is okay and typical to need to respond emotionally to an event, person, or memory several times before arriving at a place where you can let it go for good. Avoid negative self-talk or forming the opinion that you are somehow broken if you need to express the same feelings again. Try writing in a journal or finding a healthy outlet for the emotions. Relying on other people to listen repeatedly may be too difficult for them, so explore other healthy outlets for your repeated emotional experiences. It is a valid need, so treat it as such.

Discontinue any comparisons you are making between yourself and others. You are living your life right now. There is very little to gain by judging your ability to live your life well by comparing yourself to others. The only potentially helpful comparison is simply comparing the current you to a former you. However, even that comparison possibly has very little benefit if you are focusing your attention on creating a healthier you for the future. There is a lot to be gained by simply living and accepting the current moment, and how you are reacting to it.

Some ideas only continue to exist because you keep thinking about them. There are concepts that once were useful for you that are possibly not handy anymore. If you lack any recent evidence that an idea serves you in your current real world, then perhaps you should part with it. It may still be serving you in some way, but if it is not going to help you move forward towards a healthier life, the kind of life you want, consider letting it go.

You do not need to let hardships limit your future. You can dream whatever you wish. You may desire any future you can think of. Your only limitations are the laws that maintain the safety of the community we all live in and share. Give yourself permission to design a life around your passions and to keep seeking all the experiences that bring you joy, the things that motivate and drive you.

Your perspective of reality is exclusive. Part of the human experience is to live a unique life with a unique perspective on reality. Reality is just a common meeting place, not a constant requirement. You will have moments that are real that others might not experience. There is no need to panic if for a moment you experience something unique.

You are not missing. There is no need to go looking for you. You do not need to find yourself. You are here and are living in this moment. What needs to happen is that you need to spend effort creating the future you that you wish to become. Sometimes taking a vacation, a short break away from your daily stressors, might help you gain some new perspective, but such an action is not a cure all for your troubles. It does not replace taking action in your daily life. Creating the kind of life you want will happen at home, within you, and by making the hard decisions, the daily commitments to betterment.

The universe is not in debt to you. At some point during your process of growth, you may feel that someone, or even the world, owes you something. You may aim to justify that all the work you have completed and all pain you have experienced in your life is some kind of a price to pay. It is not. Sometimes life comes with a horrible experience. It is painful and it may simply just be awful. What exactly you gain from the experience is what you choose to gain from it. The universe does not decide for you when you can let go, when you can move forward. Stop waiting for some kind of debt to be paid. You can and do have the power to move forward. Compensation from the universe, the world, or any person on it is not required.

Make commitments to the real world. Watch less television, spend less time on the internet, step away from your smart phone, and limit your social media usage. You can redirect your attention to something in the room with you right now, something you can interact with, something you can experience. Focusing on the real environment around you may help you become more self-aware of your state of being. The more you know about your current self, the easier it probably is to identify what you need to do in order to increase your happiness. Be kind to yourself by showing up in the present, in the real world, and make yourself the priority you deserve to be.

Do not pick fights with your thoughts. Allow your thoughts to exist and flow. When you try to be extremely abrasive to your own mind, your mind most likely will attempt to fight back. It is okay if you need to take a couple of seconds to let a thought run its course in your mind. When the thought is over it is easier to let it go, dismiss it, or ignore it.

You may never know what caused your hardship or why it happened. Sometimes, your current self or the situation you appear to be reacting to is the result of some event or happening, but this is not always the case. Causes to your current negative mindset may never be obvious, and that is okay. Do your best to not obsess about finding a logical cause and instead focus on moving towards a healthier future.

Something does not have to have a purpose in order to matter. You may experience many things that matter a great deal, but do not really serve any purpose for you. That is okay. Some of the time, there is no logical reason why something is happening, but it still is very real. It is fine to admit it all matters. Your life matters, the events of today matter, and even your problems matter. Try to resist temptation to assign purpose to every little event of your life, just let some events simply exist. Your life can be meaningful, matter a great deal without categorizing literally every miniscule event.

You are beautiful and lovely. Being you is a wonderful experience. Today, you may feel bad, but being you is great. Stop and appreciate your uniqueness as beautiful. Question your negative thoughts about your body. Ponder the possibility that unhealthy messages may come from outside sources. Love your entire self because regardless of your body's current condition, or the current affairs in your life, you are wonderful. You always have been and always will be beautiful.

Your presence is powerful. Simply showing up to the current moment and giving it your full attention is a very powerful way of being. You can influence the present moment a great deal, even your mindset may have a huge impact. A positive attitude can go a long way to achieving a positive moment of time for you to experience.

When you hold onto anger, the only person you hurt is yourself. Do your best to realize that when you believe that you have been wronged, the best thing to do is let it go. That does not mean forgetting. It means allowing negative emotions to run their due course and let them leave. This frees you, so that you are more open to new experiences and emotions.

Bad things do not have to ruin the good stuff. What you know and believe to be good can still be good. A single bad event, idea, or object does not necessarily rob your life of any of its goodness. If one oozes into another then that is most likely a result of your actions. Choose to isolate the bad and let it go. Allow goodness to stay with you for as long as you wish it to.

Try not to rush emotions. Regardless of how you are feeling, you are probably responding to the events of your life in an authentic way on an emotional level. Allow yourself to accept that your current feelings are very real and desire to be acknowledged by you. It is okay, and often healthy to experience some sadness or grief sometimes. If you rush through those experiences, you might fail to learn what you need to grow and move forward with your life. Validating all of your emotions is often necessary. Listen to your entire self. Take care of yourself. Try your best to listen and give yourself what you need when your body asks for it. It is okay to rest, take a day off, or slow down.

You are whole and complete. It may not feel that way right now, but you are a complete person worthy of love and kindness. You may feel that you need something else, something in addition to yourself to be complete, but you do not. You do not need something outside of yourself in order to be fully human, real, and your honest self.

Replace any thoughts of needing to be perfect. You need not focus on obtaining perfection, just focus on being real. Real people have moments of excellence and periods of dullness. Real people have feelings, desires, and occasionally make mistakes. Real people, like you, can work for a better, healthier future. You deserve a real life filled with real, authentic happiness, so focus on being a real person.

Never stop learning about you, your life, and the world around you. Allow your perceptions and understanding to be changed by knowledge and experience. You deserve an enlightened human experience. Continuing to learn might result in the discovery of new hobbies, interests, and friends.

Your life's most wonderful days probably have not happened yet. You may be experiencing some of the worst days of your life. You only have the days that have already happened to you as a comparison. Imagine the future and its possibilities. You most likely have great days in your future, even the happiest day of your life to look forward to living. Current hardships might be creating the worst days of your life, but once the worst is over, you may only have the best days ahead of you.

You are not lazy. You are a person, not a single word adjective. You may have moments when you feel lazy or choose not to do something. You probably have a good reason for choosing inaction, so take responsibility for your lack of action and call it elective idleness. You are not lazy. You are just a human trying to make it through another day, so avoid belittling yourself down to a lone descriptive word. You are much more than that.

It is okay to be selfish on occasion. It is difficult for you to take care of others or complete responsibilities if you are not well. Occasionally you need to just say no to commitments and do something for yourself. Basic self-care is not a luxury, but something you need to do so that you can stay healthy. Acts of kindness towards you are a requirement for promoting good health and joy.

Your decisions have great power. Even your small decisions have the ability enhance the quality of your life. Making the decision to get an extra hour of sleep might greatly improve your wellbeing. Making the decision to bake your favorite meal might increase your happiness. Do not discount the power you have right now to increase the level of joy in your life.

Talent does not move you forward, hard work does. Stop trying to find natural abilities as if discovering them will somehow hold the answers to all of your problems. Factoring in your gifts, once you find them, is helpful, but not the solution to obtaining happiness and living a fulfilling life. Taking the time to make you, and your passions a priority will make all the difference in the world.

Identify things you are thankful for every day. Sometimes powerful changes come in small actions. Acknowledging when you are thankful takes a small amount of effort and time, but will probably create a lot of good feelings and energy in your life. Practice telling others how thankful you are for their time, help, and service. Practice being appreciative of the skills you utilize every day, your current abilities, and the resources that you have access to use. There is no need to lie or feel you must be thankful for this thing or that, but be honest. You might discover you truly do appreciate many aspects of your current self and life, maybe a whole lot more than you originally realized.

You are so much more than who you are on any single day. What defines you is a lifetime of choices. A single day in your life most likely cannot determine every little detail about the story of your life. A single failure or accomplishment is just a small part of your identity and even then only if you let it take on such worth. You have the power to decide what you believe defines you, so choose to not allow a single day in your life predetermine your future, or define your entire past.

Use failure and pain as lessons. Build upon your hardships and suffering as if they are your life's personal foundation for greatness. Learn from those experiences, if you feel there is anything to learn from them, and use that knowledge to propel yourself forward towards a more positive future.

It is okay if what you consider a priority feels unusual. You are unique, so accept that some of the things you find important are unique to you too. Being different in this core aspect makes you valuable and makes living your life exciting. Embrace your authentic self and understand that sometimes this takes you a little bit out of your comfort zone. It might feel a little bit awkward at first to make changes to your priorities, but keep pursuing your goals. As long as it does not feel extremely forced, you probably are making the right changes. Doing too much too quickly might overwhelm you, so focus on making changes to support your top priorities. Take action to be successful in a way that is most meaningful and healthy for you.

Turn a difficulty into an opportunity. It may be hard to imagine some hardships as anything positive, but the road to success is often paved with such opportunities. It is when you idle after encountering a difficultly that you will find anxiety and frustration. Look for any kind of choice, that choice is your opportunity. Through your actions, you will preserve and move forward.

Only you know you best. Being you and knowing you are two things that only you can do best. Turning to others for feedback and support is one thing, but ultimately, it is within your power and responsibility to take care of you and your needs. When there is a disagreement between your gut feelings about what you should do next, and what others in your life are advising you to do, always side with your intuition. Being your authentic self is the best way for you to feel comfortable and proud with your life decisions.

You choose your thoughts. You have the freedom and right to choose your thoughts, your reactions to the events that make up your life. You are always free to form whatever thoughts you wish to create. No one or thing can take this powerful gift from you.

Love yourself unconditionally. Accept that you are a person of great value and worthy of all the love you can imagine, no matter what actions you have taken or will take. You truly are a person of great beauty, inside and out. You always have the power and freedom to choose to think kindhearted thoughts and to shower yourself with messages of great kindness. The only time that loving yourself goes too far is when you begin to promote yourself at the expensive of others. Sure, taking care of you is wonderful and healthy, but ignoring that there exist other people on the planet too is taking it a bit far. Try your best to love everyone unconditionally, but understand that realistically the only person you can really do that for all of the time is you, and even that might take some practice, which is okay.

The future is a very real thing. Heaps of goodness can come from using your energy to focus on the present moment, but also keep in mind that you are part of the future. The future will happen, you will be an active participant in it, and a whole lot of good can come from anticipating it as the awesome, powerful thing that it is. Imagine a welcoming future where you are in a better place than today because it is a realistic possibility and you deserve to feel the joy from acknowledging its very real existence.

Take back more of what is yours. Refrain from giving away your powerful presence in the current moment. Take responsibility and ownership for all of your actions and states of being. Validate everything you are experiencing, even the bad, because it too is yours. You may be surprised by how much you really are in charge of and are responsible for, just within your current moment of existence. All that

responsibility may be scary, but more likely, once you stop to think about it, it is rather very empowering.

Accept that there will always be stuff you cannot move. There is always something in your current environment you cannot change. Often, it is the one thing you wish that was malleable, but very little good comes from feeling sorrow over the aspects of your current situation that are truly fixed. Focus instead on what is within your power to alter and then alter it. Also, accept that sometimes the one thing you can control is just simply you and the best thing to do is get up and leave. It is okay if you need to take drastic actions in order to improve your life in this moment. Listen to your intuition, your core self, your gut instincts, and that little voice inside your mind that is already providing you with the authentic wisdom that you need to hear in order to start making positive life choices to improve your life right now.

Try not to check out of the present moment. When you check out of the current moment for long periods of time, you are preventing yourself from accurately accessing the situation fully and in its entirety. How are you going to see all of the opportunities available in the present moment if you are daydreaming or reminiscing? The fact is that you cannot, so try your best to be fully aware of this moment, use all of your five senses to tap into it. You deserve to experience life to its fullest, through every sense, and throughout every hardship.

Avoid blaming the problem. Most of the time, the struggle itself is not what is problematic. How you are reacting to the existence of the struggle is usually what is causing you the most grief and suffering. Your reaction may be both emotional and physical. Listen to your mind and body. If your first reaction is to feel tense, commit to healthy actions that relieve that tension. If your first reaction is to feel angry, take healthy actions that reduce that anger.

Setbacks are only as negative as you choose them to be. It is healthy to acknowledge that a situation that is hurtful and painful is exactly that. However, there is a limit to how much good you can gain from feeling emotional pain. There does reach a point in your suffering, when you can stop the negativity from increasing, and refocus onto something more positive for you. Think about the process and journey you have endured and build on those lessons. Rebuild your life. If you need to, build it from the ground up. If it comes to it, you are much bigger and stronger than any setback. This is true no matter how long it has lasted, or how much time it has taken for your reaction to run its course.

II

<u>Realistic Changes for Reducing Stress</u>

Stress is a small word for potentially large amounts of pressure or strain that events or circumstances can place upon your physical body. There may be actions you take that generally help you feel better and relax you, but consider trying new ways to reduce stress in your daily life. A few small changes to your daily routine and habits may greatly alter how you feel.

How you need to make these changes is for you to discover, but this collection of tidbits might help you on your journey of discovery and enrich your understanding of your body, mind, and spirit. The following tidbits of optimism are meant to be reminders and advice. They are meant to empower you to form healthy responses to your life events.

◇◇◇◇◇◇◇◇

Take a minute vacation. You do not have to leave the house to have a break and relax. Take one minute and for that time think about something new and different. Try to think about something that you do not have a strong emotional reaction to yet. This way, you can even give your emotions a break, even if for just this one minute. With practice, you can extend your breaks to several minutes or an hour, but start very small. If you are having a rough day, take a fifteen second mental vacation. All aspects of you need a break from time to time, including your emotions, so give them one.

Take a new route. Leave several minutes earlier than usual and take a different route to your destination. Travel down a different street, or consider traveling by different means. You could even travel by one mode halfway there and then another mode the rest of the way. Consider stopping to get coffee or tea someplace before heading to your destination. A small change to your routine may rejuvenate you.

You are able to be selective about your worries. Just as you might prioritize your goals and dreams, consider prioritizing your worries. There is no need to worry about every single thing anyway, so just focus on a select few that really bother you. Focus on defining them. Being selective about how you describe each worry probably will help reduce stress.

Make appointments with your problems. Another strategy that might help relieve a lot of anxiety and stress is to schedule time to sit down and think about a problem. You can reserve a window of time to analyze the problem and think of possible solutions. You might spend the time brainstorming ways to find or create solutions. For full effectiveness, resist the urge to think about your problem in between appointments and define the problem in as specific of terms as you are capable.

It probably is a good idea for you to have a back-up plan. You are going to change and your priorities may change with you. When creating a vision for your future, create alternative journeys that may lead you to the same destination. Also, think about other endpoints with which you feel you may be equally satisfied. Being a little bit flexible on the details will likely relieve you of stress and anxiety too, which is a good thing for your overall health and happiness.

Create a physical space that is your retreat. You may benefit from spending some time in a calm space where you feel emotionally and mentally safe. You can create this space. Try to visit it when you need to regroup and recharge. Create a corner with your favorite chair and lamp, put up pictures that make you smile, or maybe a quiet spot with a cup of tea is all you need. Make it personal. Make it real. Retreat on a regular basis and give yourself permission to relax.

Figure out in which environment you do your best. You may need to listen to music, expose yourself to more sunlight, or warm yourself up a bit by putting on a sweater. If you have the ability, you may put up new pictures, paint a room a different color, or rearrange furniture. Discovering what you need in your environment to do your best work may lift your mood and provide you with more energy.

Exercise is great, but not the answer to every problem. Physical movement of your body will probably help you feel better. The important thing to focus on is simply movement. Try not to stress over completing traditional exercise programs. Focus on what you are comfortable doing and do what your body needs right now. If you only have the energy to walk around the block or complete some stretching exercises, then fine. Do what you can, move when you can, and give yourself a break. As long as you are trying your best, pushing yourself a little every day, then you are doing exactly what your body needs you to do.

Not all times of the day are equal. You may feel that some parts of the day are more stressful. You are not going crazy, it is a bit normal to experience stress in this fashion. Spend a few days trying to identify a pattern. You may be surprised by what parts of your day are giving you the most hardship. Your morning routine may leave you emotionally drained, so you might try eating different foods for breakfast. Your commute may cause anxiety, so you might consider trying a different route. Give yourself extra attention when you know you need it. Reflect on the possibility of making changes that continue to decrease your stress level, so you feel comfortable with your daily routines.

Cut yourself off from what drains you. You deserve relationships and commitments that bring you energy and joy. If a friendship is more draining than helpful, perhaps it is time to move onward and forward. Make time in your schedule for healthier relationships that fill you with positive energy and lift your spirits. If a hobby or social event is taking more from you than you are getting back, then it might be time to try new activities. You deserve to make smart changes at opportune times to increase the quality of your life in a manner that reduces your stress level, especially if you feel overwhelmed by unhealthy relationships.

You can do things by yourself. If something interests you, then go do it. You do not need to wait until you find someone to accompany you. You can see movies, take a walk, attempt a new recipe, start a new project, and do many more activities by yourself. It may be scary or uncomfortable the first few times, but try doing something on your own. There is no need to stress over finding a companion for activities that will make you happy that you can easily do by yourself.

Make exercising fun. Select activities that you enjoy doing. You are probably more likely to develop a new healthy habit if you find the activity pleasurable. Try new things and be open to new ways of getting up and moving. If it is difficult to find delight in any style of movement, attempt the simple act of doing something new. A novel experience may bring you pleasure and joy. Focus on finding fun and enjoyment in being active.

Listen to your body. Pay attention to warning signs. You know your body best, so take it seriously. If you know that something does not feel right, make it a priority to help yourself by providing the type of attention that you need.

You can readjust your schedule to allow more self-care, you may attempt to get a little bit more sleep, or perhaps you need to speak to a medical professional. You are your body's first line of defense, so trust your instincts. If your body is telling you something, then pay attention.

Commit to scheduling positive events. You can prioritize positive happenings by setting aside time for them in your schedule. It may be difficult to give these the same value as other obligations, but make the choice to do things for you. You deserve positive experiences and interactions. Positive events will help you stay healthy. They will help reduce your stress level.

Consider changing the relationship you have with your problems. Be honest when you ask yourself if you have a healthy relationship with your problems. You can alter how you view difficulties and the amount of negative impact they have on your daily life. A situation setting you back does not necessarily mean it has to add great stress and heartache. With practice, you can process your problems as just things that exist and minimize the amount of emotion you attach to them. You can choose to react in a way that allows you the ability to take charge, make changes, and continue onward. A little bit of stress is healthy and reacting emotionally in an honest manner is also healthy, but set a firm boundary. Make it a priority to create a method for you to respond to hardships that serves you well.

Replace time goals with actions you have control over. An easy way to reduce stress is to alter how you you're your commitment to when you are expected to be some place. You may schedule leaving your house by a specific time, but a lot can happen between the time when you wake up and the time you walk out the door. Instead, make a list of actions you want to complete before leaving and set a time for when you start that procedure. Just remember to give yourself a few extra minutes so that if something does come up, you will not feel rushed.

Be prepared for reasonable events. There are things you can prepare for without obsessing about their consequences. Keeping an umbrella in your car or purse is not a sign of paranoia but of appropriate precaution. Taking a book with you when you run an errand is a sign of smart planning, since often you may find yourself waiting in a long line. There are simple things you can do to plan ahead that are smart, sensible, and will reduce anxiety or worry.

Focus on what you can control right now. There will always be things you can control and things that you cannot. Apply your energy to things that are within your control that you wish to change. Alter them so they are healthier for you. It will take some practice, but in time, you can build a much more positive life for yourself.

There is power in giving something a name. As long as something exists in the vague world of ideas and feelings, then it may seem much bigger than it actually is. By naming something, even if it is a name that only makes sense to you, then you are taking away its power. You can start to describe it. You can start to tell its story as defined by you. You can begin to take control back and reclaim it to work into your life story as told by you.

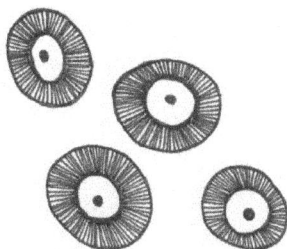

You can make your life story more positive. Perhaps you feel that your past is mostly negative or that your memories are more like nightmares. Try focusing on what you can do today, right now, to begin to create positive events in your life. Start small and in time, you will begin to have new memories to reflect upon.

Refrain from tolerating items that are not working well. You have enough to keep track of and be responsible for each day. You do not need to deal with items in your home that are not working properly. Invest in properly functioning alarm clocks, appliances, and other items that you use frequently. You deserve to live in an environment that serves you well and brings you joy. All of those small inconveniences add up to be a major stressor.

Take some time to unclutter your space. Extra stuff can add extra stress to your life. Consider owning fewer items. If the task of discarding things is too hard for you, try reorganizing the ones you have. Try relocating five items to better fit your needs. If that works well, then try five more. In time, you can work towards a better environment for your stuff, and thus, for you too.

You can schedule self-care and downtime. You can create the time to take care of yourself. You deserve to have moments when you can relax. Plan some time that you can devote only to self-care, even if it is only for a few minutes. Commit to a schedule of regular periods of downtime when you can relax. A few minutes of deep breathing, a few stretches, or a quiet minute some place where you feel comfortable most likely will help reduce stress.

Find courage to let go of the things you cannot change or control. There will always be some things going on in your life that is not within your control or power to alter. It takes life experience to know what you actually have control over, but it takes courage to make the steps necessary to change them. Practice using your courage to identify and then mold the kind of life you wish to live on a daily basis.

You do not owe anyone an explanation. You really do not. You probably do not have the energy to respond to every request for an explanation about the different aspects of your life, especially hardships or difficult situations. If you do respond to someone's request, make it simple. You are allowed to tell someone that you are busy, that you are unavailable, or that you have other commitments. You do not have to explain what you are busy doing, why you are unavailable, or what kind of other commitments you have. Frankly, that is not their business. If someone insists on knowing, he or she might not be looking out for your best interests. You are allowed to have a private life. Establishing where the boundary of your private life starts may go a long way to reducing stress.

You can be nice and forgiving to yourself. Treat yourself with compassion and understanding. Sometimes the best person to give you the type of kindness you need is you.

There is nothing wrong with that. The world has not failed you. Sometimes you are the best person for the job.

Create something tangible. Set aside time to make or build something that you can finish in a short amount of time. Do something small so that you can feel and experience what it is like to finish a project. A sense of accomplishment, even a small one, can greatly reduce stress and increase your level of joy.

View frustration as an opportunity to practice patience. Events will happen outside of your control, but you can choose to form any opinion of these events you wish. You may choose to be frustrated, adding unneeded vexation to your emotions. You may also choose to see these events as opportunities to practice being patient without letting anxiety build inside of you. Practice different ways to calm yourself into a less anxious state. Take a deep breath, refocus your attention, and strive to gain a new perspective. You deserve to be less anxious and stressed. Invest in the effort to regain a better, healthier state of being. Invest in you.

Avoid quickly accepting your assumptions as truth. It might be tempting to use assumptions as a temporary friend to get you through a difficult time. However, allowing yourself to reach conclusions without all the facts available is likely only generating more stressful thoughts in your mind. It is stressful to go about your day making decisions and choices not based on as full of an understanding of reality as possible. With every conclusion drawn from an assumption, most likely you are closing your mind off to the possibility that you need to learn more. Assumptions cannot always be avoided, so do the best you can with what is available. Just strive to make decisions based on facts as often as possible.

You can take a short break from your problems. There is no need to think constantly about what ails you. It is okay if you take a few minutes to think about some other thing or to distract yourself from your troubles. Giving yourself a brief break might help you gain some clarity about the situation.

Collect information about risks. You can prepare yourself before taking a possible risk. It is important not to obsess about preparedness. Taking the time to understand different possible outcomes might reduce your stress and you will most certainly have realistic expectations regarding how you will fare from the experience.

Prepare for the future by thinking ahead. There is no need to fixate about what may happen tomorrow. However, if you have the energy, taking a few moments to prepare may serve you well. Lay out the clothes you want to wear, double check your to-do list or calendar, and mentally walk through all the important things that you want to happen. Taking just a few moments to plan may greatly reduce your anxiety, just do not get carried away and start obsessing. You might lose track of time and you deserve to make the most of this day too.

List everything you can think of that is bothering you. Write it or type it, it does not matter, but attempt to take an inventory of all the things that seem wrong, or greatly bothers you. Afterwards, review your list and see if a pattern emerges. You may find that many of the things that bother you stem from one major stressor or originate from the same environment. Even if no pattern emerges, it may just be helpful to get everything written down.

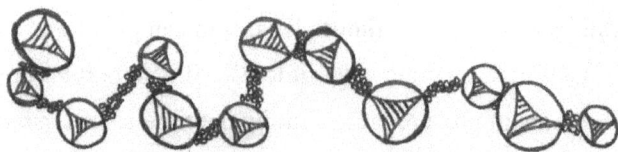

Crying is a part of the human experience. Try not to hold back tears. When you can and feel safe to do so, allow yourself to cry. Even if you are too sad to feel relief right now, a little bit of crying might help you feel less stressed and release a lot of physical tension.

Wear clothes that fit you well. You are the only one that knows which size is printed on your clothing label. Ignore the small detail of that number or letter and focus on if it fits you appropriately. Wear clothes that are comfortable so that you can focus your thoughts on other matters.

Devote time to your mental and emotional well-being. You may desire to improve your physical health, but also try to set aside time to take care of other aspects of yourself. Your mental health and emotional well-being also need attention. Practice making all different aspects of your self-care a priority.

Unplug for an hour. Turn off all electronics and refrain from using them for an hour or even a whole day. Assess how you feel afterwards. You may find that being connected to so much technology is actually depleting your happiness level. Try unplugging an hour before going to bed, or while you are working on important projects. Self-care tasks might also be easier to accomplish if you turn off your phone and refrain from using technology.

Change your environment when there is a need. Occasionally everything, every little thing, may be bothering you. If you can, remove some of the items that are bothersome. Turn off a bright light, change clothes, go barefoot, or just look in a different direction. A small change can have a profound impact, and there are small changes you can make no matter where you are. It just might take a few moments to realize what they are, and some might be hard to discover, but give it a go. It may provide a small amount of immediate relief and improve the amount of joy in your daily life.

Try identifying the source of a problem in as specific manner as possible. Attempt to pinpoint the exact cause of your unsettling mood. Identifying that the cause of your sadness is a specific song you heard on the radio is much easier to deal with than declaring all music as the source of your negativity. Identifying shoes with high heels as being bothersome to your feet is much easier to work with than declaring all shoes horrible. The more precise you can be, the easier it likely will become for you to resolve your problem and bring more glee into your life.

Do not stress about following plans exactly. Sometimes you try very hard to follow all the details of your plan, but still something unexpected happens. That is okay. Try your best to do what you can when you are able. Make peace with knowing you are doing your best.

Practice being fully present in the here and now. Being more aware of this moment will help decrease stress by limiting the amount of energy you are devoting to other moments of time and space. You deserve to experience your life to its fullest. One way is to focus on this current instant and be aware of it in its entirety. Acknowledgment of this moment of time, even if parts of it are negative to you, might bring you a lot of inner peace.

Sometimes staying busy is best. There may be times when you are so frazzled that the best way to cope with your situation is just to stay busy. Consider keeping your hands in motion by doing something safe and productive like folding clothes or doing a few push-ups. You might also try being creative and make a piece of art. Maybe you just need to do something repetitive like organizing your pantry or alphabetizing your books or movies. Maybe you just need to allow your mind to do something very boring and dull for a few hours. It is okay. Do not worry about small stuff like how weird what you have to do might seem to others. It is none of their business anyway. Some of the time, you just need to play with watercolors all night or do several word search puzzles. It is fine.

Write about what you like most. One exercise that may help relieve you of negativity is to write about what you believe to be your best quality. If it is hard to write about yourself, try instead writing about a topic you enjoy. If nothing comes to mind, then write about something new that you have not explored before, and therefore have no feelings towards yet. Explore the thought and describe it. Discuss your unique viewpoint on the matter. This exercise might help reduce stress by providing you something positive or calming to think about for a while.

Try relaxing your emotions. You may find that exercises in relaxing your physical body do not provide enough relief for you. Think about trying exercises to relax your emotions too. Remove yourself from emotional triggers. Attempt a healthy emotional release like laughter, crying, or talking. You might aim to take some time to do something quiet that you find peaceful. You may think of other healthy ways to give your emotions a break, which is fine too.

Let go of needing to identify your feelings or moods constantly. You may not know what is bothering you today. You may not know what you want to do in the future. That is okay if occasionally you simply just do not know. Give yourself a break and think about or do something else for a short while. Forcing the issue may only add unwanted negativity, so spend some time not worrying about it. Revisit the issue later.

Commit to one day of positivity. For one whole day, only post and say positive things on social media sites. Only spend time with people and in environments that give you energy. Avoid things that drain you and refrain from making negative comments. Do your best to listen to your authentic self and provide you with the kind of positive actions that you need right now to be healthy and happy.

Pause, take a break, and reflect on your recent actions. Taking time to rest is healthy. It often helps relieve stress and anxiety. Pausing for clarity is not a sign of giving up or failing. It is the action of a responsible person seeking a better way of life. There is no reason to feel guilty for taking a short break, especially if you want to quickly access if you are making progress towards a goal. Your goals are important and taking a moment to self-check your actions is also important.

Celebrate your victories. All victories are significant, so make an effort to celebrate them. Even small victories are worthy of praise. Give yourself credit when you have earned it, even for the little stuff. If it is important to you, then you should recognize it as such.

Give yourself a time buffer. Leave for appointments, school, work, and other meetings a few minutes earlier than usual. That way if something out of your control happens, you probably will make it to the commitment on time. You will feel less rushed and more in control of your life. Showing up to important events on schedule will increase your happiness.

Try not to obsess about identifying every stressor in your life. While it might be important to devote some time to clarifying what exactly is adding tension to your life, you may want to consider limiting your time trying to discover this. Instead, focus more of your attention on taking care of the version of you living in the present moment. Seek out from your current surroundings what your current self might need to be successful today.

You have five senses, not all are equal. You may have times when one of your senses is causing you grief. Ignore it and focus on another. When you can, provide yourself with the self-care you require to feel well again. If hearing music and noises brings discomfort, consider retreating to a quiet place and knitting, take on a craft project, or practice meditation. It is okay if you need to give one of your senses a break. You are not broken, you just need to focus on your needs and take care of yourself.

Consider getting rid of virtual clutter. We all have extra things that only exist in the virtual world. It is easy to simply store all of your photos, messages, and other stuff online or on a computer. However, having less virtual stuff to keep track of may reduce your stress level. It might be challenging, but start small. Consider deleting old emails or getting rid of super fuzzy photographs that are not benefiting you.

Making decisions can be stressful. When trying to create a healthier lifestyle, mindset, and sense of self, many decisions may need to be made by you. It can be very stressful, so give you credit when it is due. It is not always easy to accept and act on new responsibilities when they become available. Take time to celebrate making a selection and taking action. Take time to relax after finalizing an important decision because you deserve to enjoy the happiness you create by your choice of commitment.

Leave positive notes for yourself. Create notes with uplifting messages, even cheesy ones, and then place them so you will rediscover them later. Tape a note of encouragement on your alarm clock so it is the first thing you see in the morning. Tape a positive note on your toothpaste, so it is one of the last things you see before you go to sleep. They can be quotes from people you admire, or simple phrases of goodness. You might not believe in them in the beginning, but just seeing positive words over time might help lift your spirits.

Make your attempt to reduce stress an active one. It is easier said than done, but you might ponder that there are different ways you may be under stress. Thinking about how you are under stress and taking action to reduce it are different things. If you are unable to relieve your emotional stress right now then attempt relieving some physical stress. Try stretching or a warm bath. Calming music is helpful for some, but it most certainly will take some trial and error to discover what kinds of actions reduce stress for you. Once something works, it may not work every single time, but continue trying new ways of relaxing.

Today is a good day for change. You do not have to wait for a holiday or special occasion to start making changes towards a healthier, more positive life. It is easy to make vague promises that at some point in the future you will start a new habit or attempt a new routine. You do not need to wait for the calendar to give you permission. You can give yourself permission to start today to make the changes you need to live healthier.

It takes practice to become resilient. Things do not always go as planned and that is okay. Every time something does not go the way you want it to, you have an opportunity to practice bouncing back. With time and repetition, it will be easier to rebound after a setback. Instead of viewing resilience as a skill or talent some are just born with, consider viewing it as a skill you can develop.

Having some kind of a hobby is good. Continue to pursue old interests or take up new activities through any hardship or tough situation. As you grow in life, it is normal to discontinue old hobbies and try new things. Consider picking up new passions or developing new skills. You deserve to have comforting and, if possible, enjoyable fun habits as part of your regular routine.

Take back ownership of more of your time. There may be times during the week when you feel like you have turned over your life, but you have not. You may have to go to work, to an appointment, to run errands, but this is just part of your schedule. What you do on the journey there is also your time. You can choose how you travel, the route of your trip, and what you do while making the journey. All of that is really your time. You can choose how you spend it.

Do an everyday activity differently. You are able to influence positive change upon your everyday environment. Change how you fold your clothes. Make something new for breakfast. Use different toothpaste or experiment with different ways of cleaning the dishes. There are many possibilities to try. You might discover a method that works better for you, which you then can adopt into your daily routine.

Go outside. You do not need to have a destination in mind, just go. It does not need to be for long, even if you stand outside for a few minutes, this is good. Reconnecting with the outside world, even for just a few moments, is probably good for you. It can go a long way to reconnecting you to the world in a positive way. Try finding words to describe the noises you hear. Try identifying what you smell and taste. Focus on your senses. This exercise, no matter how brief may be very beneficial.

Have a date with your money. Make a nice meal, put on fancy clothes, and get comfortable. Spend the evening with your budget. Sit down, listen to soothing music, and go over your spending and savings. You can research ways to spend money more wisely, make lists about how you want to invest in your future, or even just cut coupons for your next grocery store trip. Reviewing your finances does not have to be a negative emotional experience.

Add variety when and where you can. Repetition might not seem like a common stressor, but too much monotony can begin to wear you down and drain you. Try to add new things to your life when you feel comfortable doing so. It does not have to be big or grand. Consider trying a new food, going to a new park, or learning a new exercise. A little variation can go a long way to increasing your joy, as well decrease unwanted stress.

Think more about the benefits of work, not how hard you work. The actual details of hard work can rob you of your desire to even begin. It is okay to think about the outcome and benefits of your work. It is fine to take a minute to imagine standing at the finish line before you start. You may feel more motivated and excited to devote the time and effort if you take a moment to remind yourself why you chose that goal in the first place.

Devote your energy to putting solutions and change into action. Refrain from using your energy to relive past negativity and repeating actions that result in unhealthy results. Make choices each day that use your efforts to their full potential and will generate the most positive outcome possible.

Give yourself a chance to recover. It is easy to stress yourself out by placing unrealistic demands on yourself to recover immediately after a setback. Give yourself a little bit of time. Recognize the setback as an opportunity to develop important skills like competence, which will form out of the knowledge that you are able to climb out of most situations on your own. Many of life's smaller disappointments can be handled well by using your own energy and smarts to heal, thus moving you forward towards your goals. Recognize your competence. Recognize the healing skills you already have.

Avoid quick fixes. Turning to a quick fix may ease your personal suffering for a very short duration. However, when you look at the big picture of your life, you will increase your suffering. Instead, practice different healing coping strategies and remedies for decreasing stress and other negativity. There is no one way that works for everyone, so give yourself a break and accept that it will take time to develop a healthy regiment of ideas and strategies to promote your long-term wellness.

Take a hard, thorough look at your current, daily actions. Consider dietary changes, new exercises, listening to new music, going for a short walk, watching a movie, or maybe taking a nice long, hot bath. Discovering more about yourself, and healthy ways to increase your wellness while decreasing tensions will make you feel better. Do not resort to quick fixes or repeatedly select actions that are do not serve your best interests, health, or priorities. You have the power to choose what you need.

Treat yourself. There is no need to wait for someone else to give you a nice present. Give yourself flowers, a new outfit, or a night out. You deserve the occasional indulgence. Just stay within your budget and make sure it will take away stress, not add to it. Make sure the action will increase your health and happiness.

Relaxation does not necessarily mean doing nothing. Taking time to relax means doing something in the moment, living in the moment and doing something that brings you joy. Seek out activities that are in themselves pleasurable, and have no rigid goals. Doing something that is open ended where you focus more on enjoying the process will aid you well and bring an inner peace that simple inaction cannot. It will also give your mind a break from taking part in goal seeking activities, and all the imposed stress attached to such commitments.

Invest in understanding where you function best.
There are many aspects to any kind of environment. Extend some effort to understand the conditions under which you function best. Do you work better while listening to music? Do you accomplish more when you are wearing comfortable socks? Try different things and experiment with what you can to discover what helps you focus and accomplish your goals. Repeat the same process for an environment where you can relax and recharge. Do your best to create an atmosphere where you can play around with hobbies and side projects that are free from your goal driven tasks. A balance of both will create a greater sense of self and increase your sense of purpose. It will also decrease your overall stress while promoting greater wellness.

Invest in supplies that help you relax. It is probably worth the time and money to invest in simple tools like art supplies, relaxing music, beautiful artwork prints, comfortable pajamas, and any other small items that you know will help you relax. Making time to recharge your energy is part of the battle to promoting a healthier lifestyle, but when you can, make small monetary investments too. You deserve it.

Reduce your stress level by eliminating competition in the healthiest manner possible. The easiest way to get rid of competition is by being your authentic self. You are unique. It makes sense that your goals and the path you need to take to get to them are also unique. The more authentic you are, the less you will need to fight or compete with others to obtain what you need to achieve your dreams because you will be the only one on that journey—your beautiful, unique journey.

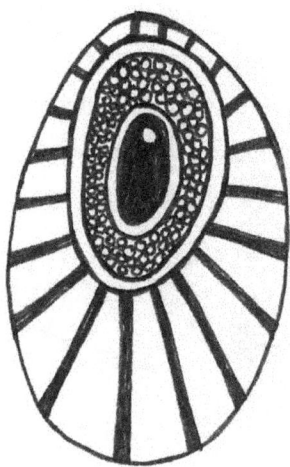

III

Living Life According to Realistic Values

One of the hardest parts of life to master is the very simple concept of forming values that you want to live your life by and actually committing yourself to the action of doing exactly that. It is incredibly challenging to prioritize all the events, situations, and feelings you experience into an easy to manage system of purpose that you can effortlessly follow every single day.

Discovering exactly what you value most out of your life experiences might be challenging. It may be a struggle for you to develop an in-depth understanding of your goals and dreams. It might also be hard for you to identify which ones mean the most to you. The hardest part is learning how to focus your energy in a way that best creates the kind life you desire. It is a task you are capable of achieving. It just takes a little bit of practice, lots of thought, and most of all, a desire to live your life better. You can make choices every day towards building a life that is a better fit for you, and the goals you intend to accomplish.

Realistic values do not mean settling for a life less than what you deserve. It means establishing a plan of action filled with love and compassion. It means reaching out towards the dreams and goals you intend to finish. It means learning how to prioritize your desires, hopes, and needs so that they become more than a realistic vision, but part of your everyday reality.

◇◇◇◇◇◇◇◇

Reexamine how you think stress benefits you. Having a lot of commitments, worries, or an overwhelming schedule does not make you more important or a harder worker. It just makes you more stressed. Avoid the temptation to put overwhelming pressure on yourself. Do your best to be your own finest friend and ease up on stress inducing expectations.

You decide your purpose. There are many things in your life you do not get to decide. You cannot choose when the sun rises, where you were born, or how others choose to respond to your actions. However, your purpose is not random. Your purpose and the purpose of all your experiences come from your choice to define one. Creating a purpose begins with you and your commitment to establishing one.

Take the time to ask if your goals are realistically attainable. You might get excited about discovering a goal that you want to work towards and forget to take a hard look at how long it might take to achieve it. You also may need to examine your abilities and strengths. You might have assumed a goal is a great short-term achievement, but when you look at it more realistically, it is better for you to define it as a long-term goal. It is okay to adjust your goal planning to fit your needs. It is an act of responsibility, not failure if you need to make these kinds of adjustments.

Be honest about why you are aiming for your chosen goals. Responsible goal planning requires more from you than just a desire to achieve. It also requires your commitment to be honest about your intent. Before investing your time, money, and energy towards a project, you can ask yourself the hard question of what your true intent is before moving forward with your plans.

Challenges may show up more than once. You have not failed if a problem shows up in your life more than once. Every so often a hardship will seem to have finally gone away only to make an unwanted appearance again later. Not all is lost. Do not give up hope because you may have to tackle a problem again. You are entering into the situation wiser this time around, so you are stronger this time too.

Choose actions that reflect your values. It is okay to have faith and beliefs. Your priorities are truly yours. Your values are for you to decide. However, having values and living your life by them are two different things entirely. Making decisions and acting in accordance with your values most likely is how you will achieve a purposeful life.

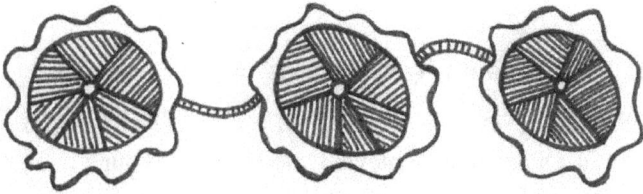

Identifying emotions is important. Discovering the emotion you need in order to accomplish your goals is necessary. A lack of resources is often an excuse given for not reaching goals, but you can challenge that idea. If you are not in tune to the emotions you need to reach the goals you have, and build the life you want then take a step back. Ask yourself what emotions you repeatedly fuel and be honest about what needs those emotions are serving. There are probably healthier emotions you can tap into which serve the same need that will also provide the support you crave. This shift of focus can help you reach your dreams and goals.

Prioritize which activities you are going to do first. It is easier to focus on your actions when you do only one thing at a time. Try to avoid distractions and interruptions. Consider turning off electronics when you sit down to read, do a craft, or do other hands on activities. When you are on a computer, try to finish reading or exploring one website or application before opening up another. It may also reduce your stress level to worry about and focus on one thing at a time.

You do not need to believe everything you think. Some thoughts may need to just pass through your mind and disappear. Not everything you come up with is useful or healthy. Focus your power and direct your energy to choose what thoughts to assign value to and which ones to dismiss. Select ideas that empower you, that reaffirm your connection to reality, or that aid you in a similar way.

Remember why you started. There is a reason you selected your goals in the first place. If you find that you are overwhelmed, remember your reasons for choosing these goals. Maybe you can now think of other reasons why you are attempting to make your life better in this specific fashion. Continue to work towards a healthier you.

Persist with your efforts to make your life more enjoyable. Reconnecting with your motivation may help you carry that purpose forward to the present and with you into the immediate future.

Pick your battles. You cannot fight every single argument or battle you are invited to participate in, so do not try to participate in all of them. Be selective about which one you are going to devote your energy to right now. Put all others off until a later time, or choose to participate in none of them at all. You have the right to choose which battles you want to partake in.

Take action to protect what you find meaningful. Identify what you value most. Then, make decisions consistently to guard your values. Be open to allowing some flexibility when you experience situations that test your values and be open to modifying them. Part of the human experience will involve change, so be open to changing the deepest, inner parts of you. You deserve to live a healthy, happy life, and this will involve adjusting your sense of self from time to time. Make the changes that are the most meaningful to you.

Identify your needs versus your wants. Spend time and effort differentiating between what you need to be healthy and what you simply just want. Be honest and real about your needs. You do need things that help your mental, social, and emotional health just as badly as things for your physical health. Practice asking for things that you need and be honest about how much you really need them. Try asking for things that you want too, but be truthful about how they are simply things you want. You may have times when you can only obtain what you need, so do not waste resources gathering stuff you want at the cost of things you need.

Take the time to define your goals. Ambiguous goals are rarely achieved because you most likely do not know what it would look and feel like to achieve them. Make it a priority to describe and define your goals. Describe all the steps you need to take in order to reach your goals and celebrate each step of victory along the way.

Select your actions based on your priorities. It is one thing to make a goal and a list of smaller sub goals to help achieve it. However, your first real test will probably be taking action based on your decision to make something a priority in the first place. The small decisions you make each day affect your future. Choose to commit to the goals you value by making choices that move you towards what you believe to be most important.

Resist waiting for an invitation to take the first step.
Most likely, you do not need to wait for someone else to give you permission to take action. You can do something right now to help ease your suffering that is both healthy and productive. Every so often, the best course of action may be just to look for new resources or ask for help. That is always okay.

Ask yourself what are the most important things that you want out of life. The answer, once you really stop and think about it, might surprise you. Devote a few minutes to trying to connect with and identify the most important things that you want. Focus on what your current life needs right now before looking into the future.

Visualize the process of living a life free from what ails you. Spend some time imaging what it would be like to live a day free from all your problems. Focus on the process of living that day. Think of all the details, the routines, the order in which you would carry out tasks. Imagine the specific actions you would choose. Consider choosing to do some of those actions today. You might discover a new method of reaching some of your goals.

Try making a list of what you do not want. Occasionally answering the question of what you want or desire is in itself overwhelming. Consider instead describing or listing what you do not want out of life, or your future. Your list may be long, but it is still an important place to start.

Practice identifying the skills you need for your goals. Deciding what goals you wish to work on is only part of the journey to achievement. Take time to list all the skills you think you might need to reach your goal and include the skills you already possess. Knowing what to practice in order to move forward towards the future you are creating for yourself is most certainly beneficial for you.

Form opinions about the details. You might not know what will increase your happiness right now and that is okay. Focus on forming strong opinions about exactly what you do not like. When you think about your job, school, relationships, and daily life, you likely will notice a few things that, to you, are especially awful. Take note of these and when an opportunity surfaces for a new job, new classes, new relationships, or a new environment consider changing to something different than what you have identified as being negative for you. After some changes, you most likely will discover something that you like more and is positive for you. Sometimes change is all you need, so look for those opportunities and try not to pass on something that will decrease your stress simply because it is not the 'big one' you were hoping to find.

Choose to be a selective worrier. There may be many things, ideas, and situations that you wish to worry about, but there is no need. Be selective about what you spend your time thinking about because you deserve to spend your time in a manner that reflects what you value. Try to focus on only one worry at a time, if any at all. You have the power to prioritize what you are concerned about and to choose to devote your time to those things.

Examine consequences. You may find that you are not sure what the next step may be. One way to determine your next action is to consider each action's possible results. While you cannot predict the future with certainty, you may find that after thinking about the cause and effect relationship of events to the end, one may appear wiser.

Free time is something you can make or find. There is no need to live your life waiting for free time to appear magically. You can schedule downtime and make it more of a priority. You have the freedom and power to make this happen. At first, you may only find a way to schedule a few minutes of free time each day, but you have the power to choose to make this occur more frequently.

Start imagining what life would be like if everything went right. Consider what it is that you actually want to have happen to you and spend some time daydreaming about it. You may want to write it all down. You may find it empowering to see your future in this positive way, even if it is for the moment a series of images and events from your mind.

Not all problems are the same. You may need a different plan of action for each hardship you encounter in life. It is normal to make modifications to your plan. You may even need to try a different routine, establish new priorities, or set new goals. Sometimes the same regimen works, and sometimes not. Do not worry if you need to attempt new things. Give yourself permission to accept the current situation and react to it the way you need to.

Accept real life examples that may contradict your worldview. Strive to live each day according to beliefs you have formed based on real life examples that you can specifically recall. Accept the challenge that new life experiences may affect your way of seeing the world. It is okay to allow your view of life to be influenced by specific real events. If you feel moved by a piece of music, great food, or a stunning sunset there is no need to dismiss it. Your worldview is in flux and it will grow, just like you.

When making a decision regarding a major life change, ask if it is the best fit for you. It is easy to be fixated on the idea that if something is good for others, then it must be good for you too. That might not be true. The best-ranked school you are admitted to might have a learning environment that leaves you feeling uncomfortable. You might receive a job offer from a well-respected company, but the schedule would negatively affect your ability to continue with your favorite hobby, health care, or spend time with family. When making the tough decisions, think about what you need, not what looks good on paper. Select what is best for you, and your life.

Change your goals when you do not see progress. It is okay to let go of goals, at least temporarily, when you are not seeing any kind of progress. You can always return to the same goal later. Work towards a different goal for a while. You deserve to see the positive results of your actions and making a goal change might be the healthiest thing you can do right now. In time, you may even decide to replace one goal with a new, different plan of action. That is okay too. You have the power to commit to goals that are both meaningful and purposeful to you.

If you do not know what you want to do, just do something new and different. Every so often, the world before you may seem vast and endless. If you do not know what will make you happy, or bring you a step closer to a healthier future, then consider just doing something very unusual. As long as it is legal, not harmful, or otherwise in itself a great hardship, trying something new may help you understand yourself more and discover what might make you happy in the future.

Express yourself in a safe and healthy manner. You can choose from a large number of positive activities to express your unique perspective. Being creative is a popular way to explore your viewpoint, but there are other methods too. Building and making anything might greatly relax you and provide a sense of accomplishment. Expressing yourself does not have to be original, like a piece of art. It just simply needs to be something that you find to be a positive experience.

Sometimes not getting what you want is actually a good thing. This kind of situation forces you to be in active decisiveness. You will have to respond, understanding that even being idle is a type of response. Your response to this disappointment potentially defines who you are as a person in ways you would otherwise never discover. By no means do you have to like or enjoy the situation you are in, but understand that you may benefit from the experience if you allow yourself to be open to that possibility.

You can be true to yourself. It is possible to spend your time doing things you may not like, but still be honest about who you are and continue to be true to yourself. Honesty does not mean telling every person every detail of your life. Being true to you means making decisions and committing to actions that will, over time, help you reach the goals you desire. As long as your daily actions are true to that, then you are being honest.

Avoid assigning value to everything. Let some people, things, and experiences just exist. You do not have to label everything as good or bad. Many things can appear, leave, and just simply be a thing that was or is. It does not need your approval to exist. You can allow all kinds of people and experiences to cross your path without your energy reacting to them. It takes some practice, but it may be very freeing not to respond to all things that happen in your life.

Letting go does not mean pretending it did not happen. It just simply means you are releasing all of that draining stress and emotion to make room for more positive stuff. It is recognizing that you deserve to live today in the fullest, free of all weighed emotional baggage.

Let your heart, mind, and soul guide you on your path to a better life. Sometimes the right thing for you to do is politically incorrect, goes against the social standard, and is questionably reckless. The truth is that what you define as right for you will always be right, no matter where the current culture stands on the issue.

Your traditions are important. Customs that connect you to your own past are part of what defines you. Practicing habits, recognizing holidays, and celebrating rituals all help create your identity. Sometimes, it is not the current ceremonial act that brings your life meaning, but it is the knowledge that your actions are part of a history of tradition that proves to you its significance. That is okay too.

Focus on possibilities, not problems. Problems and the stress they bring in your life may distract you. Take a step back from all of that and look at the possibilities that are in your life right now. Devote energy to moving towards those possibilities and making them a part of your life and future.

Define success on your own terms. You get to decide what is most important to you. Therefore, you decide which achievements are the most notable. You have the power to decide what your achievements look like and feel like. When you have reached a goal, celebrate your success.

Small things might cause big reactions and that is okay. You may have extreme reactions to small things or events. Experiencing difficult times, big life changes, or stressful situations make it difficult to prioritize what is important to you because everything might seem equally important or equally problematic. It is hard to know what bothers you the most when everything seems to be the problem. It is all right to let a small thing affect you greatly once in a while. Doing so does not mean that your personality has taken a permanent turn into drama land. It just means you need extra emotions right now to deal with something and that is fine.

Strive to be an active participant. You need to actively take part in your life plan. However, doing more things does not guarantee that you will see improvements more quickly. There is no standard formula for seeing results at the rate you wish to see them. Just focus on doing what you can when you can. The more involved you are, the more you may feel hope and optimism.

There is no need to wait for a special occasion. Wear your nice clothes, use the breakable dishes, and read that book you were saving for later. You do not need to wait for a holiday or event. Today is a great day to use the good stuff and experience the luxuries you already have. Doing so is putting your values into practice. Your actions indicate this stuff is important to you, so enjoy it.

Use any anger you have to build a better future. Behind your anger is probably a type of passion, in some form. Try not to ignore your anger, but redirect it into something more positive for you and your life. Your body might be trying to communicate to you that something is very important to you, so consider listening. Try practicing healthier ways to use your energy, consider seeking out assistance from others if there is a need, and understand that anger is an emotion worth noting, not ignoring.

Refrain from making changes just for the sake of changing things. Some things need to stay the same because they are working well for you. Only change routines, habits, lifestyle choices, and relationships when the change is needed. Avoid making changes in an effort to strive for perfection, or just to put your mark on something. Have your mark be the wisdom to leave something alone when it is serving its purpose well.

Choose to be more powerful. What you take from any given situation will empower you. The responsibility lies in you to make that choice every single day. You can choose to have more control over as much of the details as you want. It is up to you to own up to your responsibility and make the decisions necessary to live the kind of high quality life you are seeking to experience.

You do not have to build a life around what you are good at doing. What you like to do and what you are naturally talented at doing may be very different, and that is okay. You are not obligated to pursue your natural talents. Instead, think about building your life around your passions. This shift may add more meaning and purpose to your life as you work towards goals that truly excite you.

Follow up your decisions with action. Making a decision can be a stressful experience. However, that act is only the beginning. Make sure to follow up your decision making with actual actions, movement that directs you towards the future you want to live. Without that commitment by you, experiences of any kind of significant change may not occur. The high quality improvement you wish to enjoy might not happen.

Practice eliminating the 'all or nothing' style of thinking. Many people believe that their values are solid, unwavering, and ridged. Therefore, everything surrounding such values may fall into an extreme category of for you or against you. Your values are not faulty if you experience a minor life event that contradicts them. However, if you experience many examples of first hand evidence that one of your values is unhealthy for you and your life, consider revising it. You are not less of a human if you need to make minor modifications to a belief. Allow your life to transform you. Allow your beliefs to grow too.

Focus your time on a few projects. It is easy to take on many different projects, and attempt to work towards many goals at once, but do not do that. Instead, redirect your time and energy to tackling one thing at a time. There may be many things you wish to attempt in an effort to improve your life, which is good. However, try to master one thing before moving onto another. It is hard to work on several personal projects at once. It is better to complete one task than to have several dozen in progress.

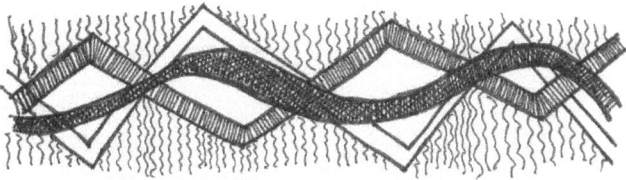

You do not have to finish every little thing that you start. Every so often, you attempt something and midway through start to realize it will bring you no joy or benefit to complete the project. Finishing might also not bring you any sense of accomplishment. It is okay to let it go. Just make sure you actually and fully discontinue the project. You deserve peace of mind. Admitting midway through projects that your priorities have changed is not an act of failure, but an act of progress. Sometimes only by doing can you learn what you value most. Sometimes letting go is a sign of achievement in itself.

Allow your passions to guide you. Being authentic about living your life according to your values means allowing your passions to help shape your goals. Be open to letting what motivates and drives you form the basis of your definition of achievement and success.

Gather information about your thoughts. Attempt to write down what you are thinking exactly. Most coping with inner angst form an extremely negative an inner dialogue. If you are able to record parts of this dialogue, it might help you identify what is most problematic. It can provide insight into your thoughts and will aid you in improving your mindset.

Make an effort to keep short to-do lists. When your to-do list is long, it may be hard to focus on seeing a task to completion. Instead, try keeping two lists. One list could be your long-term goals. The second list could be much shorter, just a few items. Reference the shorter list daily.

Once you finish a task, you can celebrate your accomplishment and then add a new goal. Narrowing your focus in this manner helps prioritize what is most important to you.

Honestly, ask yourself what is your intention. Identifying your plan and your purpose is a big part of the battle with yourself. It might be hard to articulate a specific goal or put into words your life's purpose. Focus instead on just identifying your intent. Do you intend to help others? Do you intend to be highly educated? Do you intend to eat better? Collect this knowledge about yourself and work from it to design a plan of action that you are proud of devoting you time to achieving.

Practice making selections that bring you joy. Once you have identified something as pleasant for you, be consistent in your decisions. When you have a choice, pick what you deem to be good. The more often you make selections that seem worthy to you, the more value you will begin to experience in your life.

Be in charge of something. Part of putting your values into practice is to seek out, volunteer, or create positions of leadership where you can instruct and lead others. If you greatly value sports, then consider leading a local team. If you greatly value music, consider starting a band. If you greatly value fine cooking, then consider writing a cookbook or starting a blog. Taking on such a role is not about increasing income, but about increasing your opportunity to practice something you love and value. Let the act of such a commitment be its own reward.

Stick with something even after you master it. As long as you enjoy an activity, consider pursuing it. Strive to find activities that bring you joy. It may be work, it may not be. It may be something you do once a month. Whatever it is, keep doing it. Keep cooking, keep typing, keep running, keep reading, and keep practicing and most of all, keep going. You deserve to experience that feeling of doing your personal best at something.

Realistically ask yourself who you need to become in order to achieve your goals. It is okay if you are not the person you need to be in order to overcome your current hardships and fears. Take actions every day, which over time will result in the growth and creation of the person you desire to be in the future.

Commit yourself to consistent action. It is through repeated and consistent decision making that you will reach your goals. Aim more for consistency and less for dramatic, sudden actions. The occasional big act will not benefit you as well in the long run as simply just living your daily live with consistent commitment to you and your dreams.

Frustration provides unique insight. Stop yourself from discounting frustration as only a negative state of being. There is a reason you are frustrated. Do not discount it or dismiss it. Instead, listen to it. Then, take action. Your actions dictate your future. If being stuck in rush hour traffic frustrates you, look into leaving your house a little bit earlier, or take a different route to work. If making a cake from scratch frustrates you, then buy one. There are many actions you can take that will improve your daily happiness.

Try not to confuse interest and commitment. Being interested in overcoming your current situation and being committed to overcoming your current situation are very different actions. Interest typically is internal, which is good, but only to a limited capacity. After a while, you truly need to act on that interest if you wish to see success, achievement, and movement forward towards the future you want to build for yourself. By taking action, making a commitment to your dreams, you will begin to see more positivity and success in your daily life.

Practice acts of kindness every day. A simple way to put your values into action is by completing simple acts of goodwill towards others. Feed a parking meter, hold a door open for someone, smile and greet a stranger who you pass on the street, or any other small act you can think of that reflects your values. It can go a long way toward improving your moods and living a life you consider noteworthy.

Build your confidence. It may seem like a daunting task, but with daily practice, building your confidence is possible. Allow your intent and priorities to guide you towards what you feel are the most important actions in your life. Then, use that insight of yourself to help you to brainstorm problem-solving strategies when hardships arise. After acting on self-created solutions that both work and align with your values, you will, in time, build more confidence.

Increase your integrity. Many may believe that living your life along a kind of moral code is something you cannot achieve unless you have been doing so your whole life. However, that is not really the case because it is not too late to get started. Develop a set of morals and values rooted in your real life. If in the past you were hurt by violence, you may choose to live a non-violet life as part of your moral integrity. You can create the moral code by which you want to live your life. Through your daily actions you will build as much integrity as you wish.

Be mindful about how and when you spend your time and money. Allow your spending to be an extension of your values. If you find violent movies to be repulsive, then do not buy movie tickets to see such films and do not spend your time watching them. If piercings and tattoos go against your beliefs, then do not get them. It may seem like a simple concept, and it is, but putting it into practice all of the time, not just when it is obvious or convenient, can be a challenge.

You will find as much purpose as you seek. If you search for a reason to exist, you will find one. Your purpose, your life's purpose is formed out of your decision and action to create it, make it real, and to admit continuously to its powerful existence.

Do not settle out of convenience. Try your best to make the most of all of your opportunities. Take actions and accept offers that inspire you. Even if presented with a set of options that are not thrilling, odds are that one of your current life choices on some level fills you with joy or passion. Act on the opportunities that inspire you.

Think about the longevity of your actions. When forming your values, consider how your decisions today will affect the future. Consider making contributions that will leave behind a type of legacy, a gift to future people, even if on a small level like your own children and their children. There are many ways to do this. Consider leaving behind something you create, like artwork or hand crafted furniture. Maybe you want to leave behind some money in the form of an inheritance, or perhaps you want to write stories and share ideas. The details are not especially important, just think about leaving something, giving something to the future. Thinking about this might help guide you towards forming a healthy relationship with your goals.

Use your imagination to serve you well. Allow your imagination to flow. Let it generate ideas and take note.

When you give yourself the freedom to thoroughly explore ideas, you may discover new interests or reignite a desire for your passions. Listen to your intuition or gut instinct. Devote your energy and imagination towards goals that interest you.

Promote and acknowledge what you love. Potentially, you can extend a lot of your energy bashing what you dislike or disapprove of. However, a much more efficient and healthier way to use your energy and power is simply to foster and endorse what you value.

Review how you define 'trigger'. It may be the case that you currently view a trigger as a bad thing, as in your bad mood was triggered by an argument you had this morning. Another way to view the ideas of triggers is to accept that it might also be one of your values, and it might actually be a positive thing for you. You may have found yourself in an argument over a desire to eat breakfast before doing your daily chores, running errands, or getting dressed. Perhaps this might tell you that you consider eating well and taking care of that need of yours first one of your values, or at least something you really want to make a priority. Allow that value to drive you and motivate you to take action and invest the time and energy to obtain it in a positive manner, without resorting to negative communication habits or unhealthy actions.

Seek out opportunities for meaningful participation. Part of living your life aligned with your realistic values is putting your values into action. Spend some time pursuing interests and volunteering for different services in your community that are meaningful to you. If you value the welfare of animals, consider volunteering your time participating in local fundraisers to help local animal charities. If you value preserving nature, consider spending time picking up a local park. You have the power to choose meaningful actions that reflect what interests you and inspires you.

Let go of assumption that the world will always guide you. If you sit and wait for permission to move forward and live your life according to your values, you might be greatly disappointed. Instead, create your own motivation by creating your own consequences. In this way, you are generating a tiny amount of positive stress to push yourself towards one of your goals. Create a self-imposed contract in which you promise yourself that if you do not devote time and energy towards the process of working towards one of your goals, then a reasonable and realistic penalty of your own creation will be imposed. You are capable of self-discipline, and sometimes the small stuff is the greatest motivation, like television watching, music listening, or dessert eating. Just keep in mind, you can be compassionate towards yourself, be flexible, and it might take some trial and error to find what works best for you.

Identify the passion behind rage or resentment. You may find yourself getting irritated about a situation. You can use that emotion to benefit you. Your strong reaction took a lot of emotional energy. Underneath all of that is a large amount of drive and motivation. Take a step back and really ask yourself why you are so upset, what value has been not been met. Allow your annoyances to help guide you towards being more authentic about what you care about and take action to live your daily life in support of these values.

You can work smarter, without working harder. There are limits to the amount of energy you are able to devote to something. Refrain from putting yourself down because you cannot do more. Instead, refocus your energy more intelligently by shifting your attention to what you believe is the most important use of your time.

You do not need more money, more time, or more energy to get started on your goals. Try your best to put a stop to this line of thinking because it is not helping you move forward towards a better life and a healthier you. There is a difference between having a goal to make more money, schedule more free time, or to use your energy more efficiently and claiming that you need money, time, and energy to make your goals happen. You do not. Stop using your current situation as an excuse not to take actions to move forward. Instead, look at your current situation and build upon it the foundation you need to start to move towards your goals and dreams.

Deadlines are rarely reflections of achievement. You are much more valuable than any set goal or deadline. Your value does not diminish because you did not meet an objective by a predetermined timeframe. Sometimes, other people may feel it is necessary to reward you for doing good work quickly, which might be okay, but when you step back and view your life in its entirety, such things are probably less important. Instead, consider whether you enjoyed working on the process of completing the project and if you felt your efforts were a good use of your time and energy.

Modify how you react to your complaints. By itself, a complaint is just an idea or an opinion. A complaint is not change. Change is the result of action. If you desire to live your life with more abundance, happiness, and with improved health consider altering your relationship with complaints. Give your opinions the credit they deserve and start taking action. Commit to the kinds of actions that will result in improvements you can personally experience and benefit from. Commit to changes you will personally enjoy. Do not settle for less by filing a complaint and not following through with some kind of productive action.

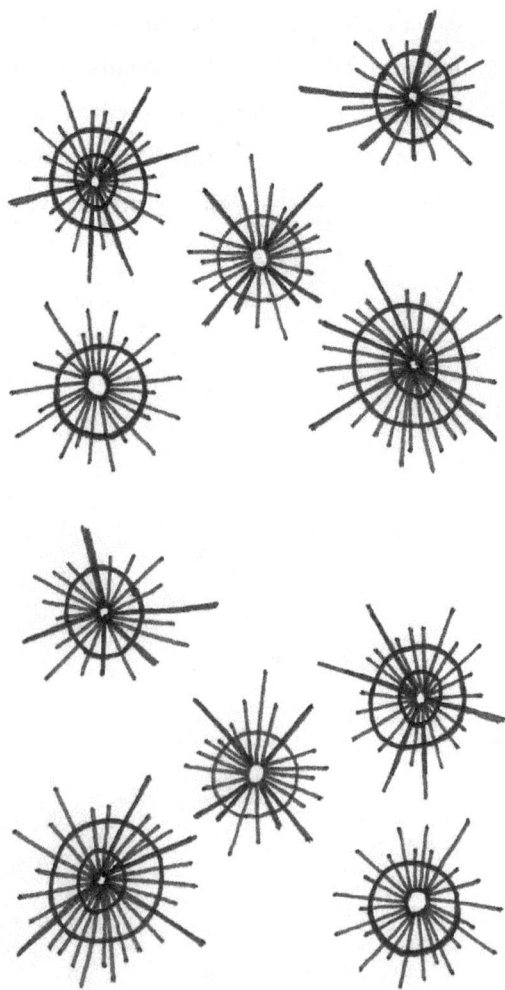

IV

<u>Setting Realistic Expectations</u>

Expectations come from somewhere. They are taught, they are inherited, and they are learned. You have the ability to recreate your expectations about everything around you, including yourself.

This section of tidbits provides many ideas about how to think about you and your future. Not just in a general sense of how you view your own future, but also what you expect out of the universe around you.

There is a difference between setting high expectations and setting unrealistically high expectations. You can both build an understanding of what exactly the universe is capable of and choose to yearn for the best it can offer you. Desiring everything all of the time will burn you, rob you of all your energy, and slowly erode your value. Instead, read the following perspectives and insights to help you find a more healthy way of being.

You deserve to look ahead in your life with optimism grounded in a foundation of truths. You decide what you value, what you believe to be the best use of your time, and how you want to react to your life on a daily basis. Make the comment to move your authentic self forward by taking action. Choose to find hope in the very real truth that you are always worthy of the best life you can create. It is a big responsibility, and at times a scary responsibility, but one that you can handle.

◇◇◇◇◇◇◇◇

There might be a delay between making changes you need to improve your life, and actually experiencing improvement. If you know you are doing what you need to do then give yourself a break. What you are trying to change, be it your body, your environment, or your quality of life may need some time to react positively to the wonderful work you are doing.

Let go of how it is supposed to be. It is easy to be stuck on a concept of how your life should be, how your career should progress, and how your current situation logically is supposed to exist. Focusing on this style of pity is only weighing you down and preventing you from moving forward. It is challenging to rethink your situation, but allow your current self to simply exist instead of accusing it of not existing correctly according to some invented ideal. This will greatly free you.

Understand there will always be things that are unknown. No person knows everything, nor does any philosophy or religion. You are allowed to react to the unknown any way you want. You can pray more, read more, think more, or ignore it all. It is up to you to decide how much value you want to place on what is unknown to you. You have the right and power to do so.

Take a look at the whole picture. Avoid letting one small event ruin an otherwise very good day. Everything may go as planned and then you encounter a snag, a small wrinkle, a tiny event that potentially could offset you, but do not let it. Let go of the small stuff and focus on the bigger event that is your day, your week, and your life. You are not a failure if one small mistake or unpredictable mishap occurs.

You may have to settle temporarily and that might be okay. You may have to take a job that is not exactly in your field of interest, you may have to live in a neighborhood that is not located in the best spot for you, or you may have to finish completing an education that you wish you could just avoid entirely. Sometimes you are on a life path that needs to happen, but it is a temporary stopping point for you to reestablish your goals and priorities. You have not failed and you are not stuck. Take pride in the income earned, the safe home you create, and the new knowledge you acquire. When an opportunity surfaces, take the next step.

Try not to pass on an opportunity just because it is not ideal. You may have an idea in your mind about what your path to your ideal future looks like. Be open to small changes and alternative ways to achieve what you want. If you wait around for what you think is the perfect opportunity, you might miss out. Consider your options. There are probably many ways to make progress and move forward in the direction you want to go.

All you can realistically ask for is an opportunity. Let go of the desire for retributions and compensations. Instead of yearning for a raise at work, look for an opportunity to request one and make a case that you deserve one. Instead of seeking out ways to hurt someone who may have hurt you, look for an opportunity to meet with and form new relationships with healthier people for you. Instead of quitting a project important to you, look for an opportunity to work on it in a different environment or with different tools. There are many ways to alter your relationship with your goals so that what you are seeking are opportunities for change. Not all opportunities will result in the kind of change you want immediately, but that is the point. All you can realistically ask for is that opportunity to take action, which is the part you can control. You cannot always control or rely on your actions to produce the kind of instant change you want, and that is okay.

It is okay if you are scared. Sometimes scary things happen to you, so being fearful is a good sign. Being healthy means a lot more than just feeling well, it also means you react emotionally to life events in a way that makes sense to you. If something scary is happening, it most certainly makes sense that you are scared.

Let your fear work for you. Making big changes often is scary because it usually takes you outside of your comfort zone. It is natural to fear those first few steps, the first decisions that you need to make, and the first actions you want to commit to, so that you move forward and onward. Listen to your inner strength and intuition, and accept that a small amount of fear often comes with big life changes, even the positive ones for you.

You will learn a lot over the course of your life. Do not feel guilty about knowing something now that you did not in the beginning. You cannot go back in time and tell a previous version of yourself the new information. It is best to promise yourself that you will use the new information in the future. As you learn more about your situation, you will get better at taking care of yourself, and providing the kind of love you need to thrive.

It is okay to fail, especially when trying something for the first time. Expecting that the way to know if something is a good fit for you is that you will never fail at it is unrealistic. Failing occasionally, even at your talents and passions, is part of the human experience. Attempt to learn from your failures and keep moving in a general forward direction towards the kind of future you want to live.

You must accept reality, but you do not have to approve it. Reality has existed and will continue to exist as its own entity. It will not wait for your permission to press on forward. Your unique perception of reality is simply the version special to you, which you also do not need to feel pressure to approve of either. You can release yourself from that burden.

Write your own definition of success. Avoid allowing expectations invented by other people dictate what your success should look and feel like. You have the power and the right to decide when you are successful. Your achievements are met when you say they have been. You are successful when you believe to be so.

It is okay to be wrong. You may spend a lot of time fighting to be correct and right about what is happening in your life. However, insisting on being forever right is also insisting on being perfect, which is not a very healthy mindset. It often is better to accept when you really are wrong because you can more easily forgive and be open to changing what you need to. If you did not stop at a stop sign while driving, admit to it and if you need to, pay the ticket. If you broke your friend's casserole dish because you were not being careful while carrying it, tell him or her that you are sorry and offer to buy a replacement. This act of acceptance and ownership is a type of responsibility that you can put into practice daily. Often, it takes far less energy to just be responsible for your actions instead of trying to pretend you have never made a mistake. You have lapses in your judgment occasionally. It is okay. It is part of the experience of being a person.

Happiness is the result of many of your actions. One single life change probably will not bring more happiness into your life, but making several changes might. Happiness is also more than a frame of mind or collection of positive thoughts. Thinking more positively can go a long way to relieving much suffering, but you will find that your actions also play a huge role in the quality of your life.

You may still face difficulties after doing all the right stuff. There is no guarantee that by doing everything in your power to do that you will reach your goals without any kind of difficulty. Realistically, you probably will have some difficulties. However, resist the urge to stop. Press forward and onward. Keep doing what you need to do to build a life you are proud of living. The path to a healthier life may be filled with an unfair share of misfortune, but that does not mean you are doing anything wrong or that you are a failure. Keep doing what is right for you.

The world is not ending, it just might seem that way. Tomorrow, this beautiful lovely planet Earth is still going to be here. You lack the ability to destroy it. You really do not have a personal relationship with Earth's future. Nothing you can say or do is going to cause the world to self-destruct. Go ahead, live your life, and understand it is okay if you make mistakes. Your mistakes will not irreversibly harm the universe. You have a lot of power, but not *that* kind of power.

Only you can move yourself towards an opportunity. Others may provide an opportunity for you, but it is your choice and your actions that will help you succeed. Try not to wait too long to take advantage of it. Ask for help if you need it, but remember, it will be you that takes the first step and sees it through to the end.

Success is not a road paved with perfection. A common misconception is that only perfect deeds result in excellence, but this is often not true. Your path to overcoming any hardship and reaching the kinds of success you want will probably include a variety of events. Some actions you will complete efficiently, some may be spectacular failures, and some might be moments of brief misdirection. Your future is an exceptional path that you travel. Embrace its uniqueness.

Try not to obsess over avoiding negativity or failure. Bad stuff will still happen sometimes even when you work very hard and put forth a lot of effort. You are working hard to improve your overall quality of life. That means it is okay if something bad happens occasionally. A small setback does not mean you have failed at you quest for a better, healthier life.

People get to think what they want about anything and everything—including you. How you think is your business and your private affair. At the same time, it is not your business what or how other people choose to think about anything, including you. That is, if they choose to think about you at all. Let go of any expectations that you must know how often and in what ways another person thinks of you. Instead, just practice being more mindful about how you think of yourself.

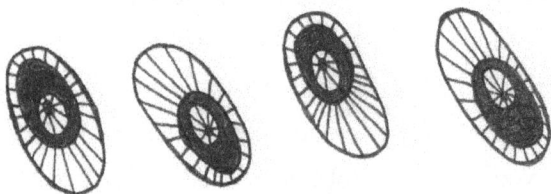

Our problems are unique, so are our solutions. What works for someone else might not work for you. That is okay. You do not have the find the same pieces of advice useful, the same religious practices uplifting, or experience the same kind of happiness. It is okay to seek out solutions that work best for you.

You have the right to find zero purpose in your suffering. You can choose to write it off as a no good, very bad time and continue on the same life path you had before you had these current hardships. Not everything you experience in life has to be soul changing. There is no reason to feel guilty for not being more swayed by your situation. Sometimes there is no point, cause, or lesson that you feel worthy to take from a life experience and it is your right to form that opinion.

Do the most you can with what you have. Think about reevaluating how you are using the resources to which you currently have access. You may find that you can do a lot just by making small changes with the current tools at your disposal. You may not need all the stuff you yearn for. There often are many ways to attain a goal, so keep an open mind and reevaluate what you have. With practice, being more efficient and resourceful will become habit.

Tomorrow may not be better, but it will be different. If today is overwhelming you, take comfort in knowing tomorrow will be different. It may not be as different as you want it to be, but you will have new opportunities, new feelings to deal with, and a new chance to make some changes. You may even have more control over what is happening. Take a deep breath, hang on, and wait for a new day.

A hardship changing you is not a sign of defeat. There is no right or wrong way to be affected by the events of your life. You may be a very different person, or you may not be. Accepting that there is no correct way to be altered by the experience is the healthiest thing you can do for yourself.

Contemplate changing your attitude about what fair looks like. You might be fighting to receive the same resources and opportunities as others, but you may be reaching out for the wrong type of support. It might not be what you need. Fair is getting what you need, not necessarily getting the same as others. Since you are unique, what you need is probably also unique.

Your past does not shape your future happiness. You are not destined to a future with a limited selection of moods and attitudes as determined by your current situation. Allow your future to exist as the unwritten entity that it is without any assumptions imposed onto it before it has a chance to make an appearance.

Fail better than you have ever before. Trying to avoid failure is not the healthiest of habits. In your life, you will undoubtedly try new things and most of the time you will make a few mistakes on your way to mastering new skills. You can practice failing better so you that get more out of each failure. When you fail, you can focus on what you have learned, what aspects of the situation you can improve upon next time, and reassure yourself that you are still a great person despite something not going the way you want the first time around.

Life may not provide an obvious right choice. Ideally, we want our array of choices to include one that is obviously fantastic. However, often this is not the case. Occasionally we will have to select between an option that is bad and one that is even worse. Do the best with what you are given and choose the best option available. It is the most you realistically can do, so be at peace with that.

Refrain from trying to buy happiness. There is no amount of money in the world, and no magical amount of stuff that will banish all of life's hardships. That is simply not how the human experience works. Often, the way to happiness is both simpler and friendlier to your bank account. Practice healthy habits with a positive attitude. In time, happiness will find you.

You have limits, but over time they too may change. The kinds of things that are holding you back now will probably be different in the future. Assuming a goal that is not possible today will also be impossible in the future probably is unrealistic. The future version of you might be able to handle your goal just fine.

Hardship, pain, and struggles often are not personal.
Problems are not living things that looked you up, hunted you down, and targeted you. You are simply dealing with negative stuff right now. For you to attempt to answer the question of why will only hold you back, slow down your healing, and growth process. Do your best to accept that this situation is not a sign of anything more than the fact that you and it exist.

Self-care does not need to be productive. At times self-care is all about recovery, self-preservation, or just monitoring. There is no need to pressure yourself into setting goals while you are trying to relax. You do not need to be productive or achieve anything while you are experiencing some down time. Just be kind to yourself and try to unwind.

There often is more than one way to get your needs met. You are capable and creative enough to invent new ways to meet your needs. You have the power to try alternative methods of satisfying them without resorting to unhealthy means to do so. It may take time and energy, but you deserve it.

Some change is not going to ask for your permission.
Each day brings new opportunities and new circumstances. These are not going to wait for your approval to happen. It

might be scary, but it is also exciting. Be open to unexpected change and do your best to remain flexible and resilient.

Step outside of your comfort zone, but think small.
There is no need to sprint away from what makes you comfortable. However, in order to make the kinds of changes you may need in order to progress towards the kind of future you want, some movement by you is required. If something scares you, take small steps to overcome your fear. If something causes great anxiety, then consider small exercises to begin to overcome it. In time, you can expand your comfort zone to include the environments and tasks you need to achieve the kind of life you desire.

Failure is not the opposite of success. Actually, it is often part of success. The road to accomplishment is not straight and steep. On occasion, good attempts will fail fabulously. Learn from them. Carry that vast knowledge with you forward onto greater ways of doing things.

A little guilt is okay. Sometimes you feel guilty because you committed an act that went against your beliefs. You might feel some guilt, which will encourage you to make amends with that wrongdoing and move on with your life.

When your guilt is so massive that you stop treating yourself with respect and kindness, then that is less okay.

If you want something different, you will have to do things differently. It may feel comfortable and safe to do the same things repeatedly, but only by taking the initiative to do something new, and most likely outside of your comfort zone, that you will experience growth. Rare events may happen that might alter the course of your life, but for progress towards a healthier and happier you, the events that happen will most likely originate from your actions.

List the benefits you will experience once you reach your goal. It might be helpful to write down the benefits you expect to receive next to your goals. You may want to incorporate these benefits into your decision to select one goal over another. Defining the outcomes you anticipate, even for small daily goals, may motivate you in ways you previously never imagined.

You may need to modify your beliefs and that is okay. You may need to rethink your worldview a few times, especially as you grow and change. You might experience some things that challenge your understanding of the world. It is normal and healthy to allow your personal experiences to alter your understanding of the universe. It is not a sign of going crazy, but a sign of responsibly. You are adjusting to your current self and life.

Feeling happy is not being happy. It is possible to use medications or drugs to produce chemical reactions that would cause of a variety of positive feelings, but that is not to be confused with actually being happy. Happiness generally is the result of a lifestyle of healthy choices and is built over time. You have the ability to make daily changes by starting small and working towards improving your whole life so that you may experience happiness more often.

Let go of the idea of perfection. You might yearn for something to work perfectly or be perfect, but it most likely is not the best of ideals to hold on to in your life. Each time something in your life does not meet your high expectation of perfection, the disappointment probably adds stress. Consider rethinking how you view your job, your projects, your beliefs, your relationships, and even yourself. Shift the focus from perfect to just healthy and ask if your job, project, belief, relationship, or self-image is healthy for you.

Avoid trying to stop behaviors. Instead, replace them with healthier habits. Your behavior is serving some kind of a need, so when you discontinue it without another behavior in its place to meet that need, you will start to suffer. All that extra suffering will result in your inability to maintain your goal to discontinue the bad habit. Focus on the addition of more positive ways of acting and being. Consider taking the time to identify what need that unhealthy habit is serving and practice a better way of living to achieve the same end.

It is okay to not be good at something. It is common to be good at some things and not so good at others. It is also common to learn quickly in one area, but not so quickly in another area. If it takes you more time than you would like to develop a skill, do not worry. It may just be a skill area where you need more time to mature. This does not mean you are broken, it just means you are a typical person. There is no shame in needing to work longer than you desire at a task. It happens. It is okay.

You are never too old to dream a new dream. No matter how many years you have been on the planet, your age is really just a number. Live past this idea of a number and dream away. Set new goals, plan for new accomplishments, and begin taking action. You deserve to be as big of a dreamer as you want and set the goals you desire to achieve. You have that right, all you need to do is give yourself permission to experience and own your desires.

Consider removing the phrase 'should have' from your vocabulary. Telling yourself that you should have done this or that implies that you are now less human because you were unable to do this thing you told yourself you simply 'should' do. Instead, describe your desired actions as things you want to do or something that you would like to do. There are many ways to express or think about your intentions.

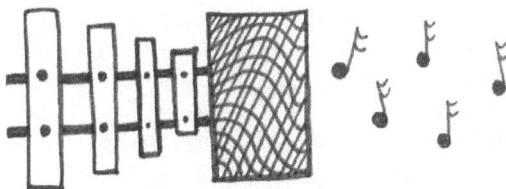

Take the time to say good-bye. Making the decision to let something go may be very good for you, but so is taking the time to say a proper good-bye. It is important to acknowledge all the time and energy you spent on something, even if it will no longer help you in the way you need in the future. It is okay to say a proper good-bye to something, a person, or an idea. Your life, all parts of it, deserves that kind of validation by you.

Sometimes you have to be your own knight in shining armor. It is okay to be your own savior, victor, or bringer of all that is good and wonderful. You can create a

119

healthier life without waiting for anyone's permission. All you need to start moving forward is your own commitment to the goal of positive change.

The road to change is not straight and steep. When you start to experience more positivity, it likely is not going to be steady and constant at first. You may perhaps still have bad moments when you feel awful while overall, you see improvements in your daily life. Accept that these are just minor events and try not to give them too much attention. If you overreact, you can cause unjustified suffering by entering into a negative mindset. Acknowledge that you are having some thoughts you do not approve of, make adjustments, but continue to move forward.

It is okay if you want something clarified. When something is confusing or you feel you do not have all the information, know that you have the power to understand more by seeking out better knowledge. Not understanding something the first time does not mean you are dumb or a bad listener, it just means that you need to seek out different or new information. There is nothing wrong with that.

Productive and busy are often two different things. Both consume lots of your time and energy. When having a bad day, either is good, because they both help you cope.

However, when looking at the big picture and long term goal planning, you want to strive to be productive and not just busy. You want eventually to develop habits that lead you to finishing tasks and projects because this will help you stay healthy.

You can be your own role model. There is no need to look outside of you to find a hero. One exists inside of you right now. Give yourself power and responsibility to rise to the occasion. You have the right to stand up for yourself and bring order to your own life. The only superpower you need is a small bit of courage. You can take the first step and practice moving forward in the direction you want to go.

It is okay to be lost while traveling in the right direction. There is no need to insist that you know every detail of your journey. As long as you are moving forward in the general direction that you need to end up, then it is fine. Allow today to be detailed and specific, but refrain from obsessing about needing that same level of detail about your distant future.

It is all right to not know what you need for your future. You will not know everything you want to know or feel you need to know and that is okay. You can make goals and work towards a better future without knowing everything. It may be scary, but you can create the life you want and make changes without having everything figured out beforehand.

Sometimes things do not go according to plan and that is okay. You can research and carefully list the best way to achieve something. You can do everything on your end perfectly, but it still does not turn out the way you want. It is a big world. There are things outside of your control. You are not a failure if something unexpected happens. You did nothing wrong.

Personal passions are found through action. The best way to discover your talents is by doing things. Try something new that you think you might like. It is difficult to know if you will enjoy something unless you actually do it. Thinking about it, talking about it, and even planning for it are all very limiting. When you take on the responsibility of action, you are actually experiencing your desires. Through the experience of action, you can more clearly define what drives and motivates you.

You can be open to change. There is a lot of truth to the idea that the only constant you can count on is change. Just as happy feelings go away and fun experiences end, the same is true for sad feelings and unhappy events. When life is good, be thankful. When your life is in some way disappointing, know that this too will change. In time, it will be different. Allow yourself to be open to that possibility.

Everyone misses a mark occasionally. Part of the human experience is to learn from mistakes, missed opportunities, and mishaps. Hard times might make rebounding from these situations difficult but keep in mind you are not the only one struggling. It is normal to reach for a goal and fall short the first time you try. Ask yourself what you learned from that experience and move forward.

Do not assume the future. Things change and are every so often unpredictable. Assumptions add stress. Assuming today is going to be awful when you have only been awake for a few minutes will probably not help you. Assuming tomorrow will be a bad before it gets here undoubtedly is not healthy. Keep an open mind about what the future may bring.

Taking a step back is not quitting or failure. It is okay and perfectly normal to step away from the current situation and look at the big picture. At times, you may need to step back or reverse a decision so that you can move forward in a better direction. The path to a better, more healthy future is not going to be a constant road of improvement. You may encounter times when things are not working and that is okay. It is not a sign that improvement is not possible. You have done nothing wrong. You just might need to make a small change.

Yes, language is sometimes limiting. Sometimes it is hard to find words to express your situation. You are not going crazy and most find it frustrating to talk to others from time to time. Focus on what you can express or consider simply investing time in an activity to help you process your stress alone. Some find journaling, light exercise, or calming music helpful. Do what you need to do to take care of yourself and refrain from having an expectation that all at times you should be able to articulate yourself perfectly.

Create a dream board or collage. It can be difficult to understand how making small changes today can impact your future and make it better. Imagining what kind of future you want is a good exercise. Sometimes making an actual physical dream board, or notebook, filled with drawings, pictures, and short descriptions of the future you want is helpful. When you can visualize the future you want to build for yourself, it will likely be easier to make decisions today that take you towards that goal.

There are no shortcuts. Change will most likely follow effort and work done by you. You are most likely going to need to comply with some kind of a plan over a length of time in order to experience improvements in your life. The situation you are experiencing will not simply vanish if you ignore it long enough.

Your situation might be a big deal. It might change you a lot. Be prepared to come out of it with different interests and opinions. It is okay if you favorite food or color has changed. Do not attempt to return to who you were before this big life-changing event happened. Instead, move forward towards a reinvented, stronger version of you.

Practice will pay off. Just as an athlete or a musician must practice daily in order to improve at their craft, you might need to now practice new skills daily. It is not beneath you, or a sign of failure to make it priority to practice new habits. By taking the time to form new, healthier habits, you can begin to create a healthier life. Coping with and recovering from a negative situation is going to take some work. It is by practicing a consistent, steady routine of healthier behavior and thoughts that you probably will, in time, start to feel and experience more positive joy and optimism in your life.

Sometimes it will not work. You may follow a plan of action exactly, and it still does not work. That is okay. It is also okay to get frustrated. Learning how to cope with and work through hardships is not an easy process. You are probably going to attempt things that work well for others, but not you. Keep trying because there are many ways to combat the various problems that surface during any human life. Through trial and error, you will find what works best for you.

Just because a problem is complicated does not mean its solution has to be. Try your best to be open to all kinds of remedies to your hardships. You may discover that it takes a lot less effort to relieve you of suffering if you are willing to let go of your expectations regarding how much effort you must put into a workable solution.

Frequently seek out evidence of your beliefs. As you grow and change, parts of your belief system or worldview might not be serving you anymore. You may also form very strong beliefs based on your feelings around specific people, things, or environments. Be open to obtaining information that validates your beliefs. Questioning your extreme emotional reactions may build confidence.

Not every day is going to be a day of progress. There will be horrible, awful days that seem to be the worst things you have ever experienced. Believe it or not, but every individual that has experienced extreme hardship has had these kinds of days. Really, every single person has.

The road to a more healthy mindset and life will likely have some of these days. You most likely will have moments when it seems like you have made no progress, but you undoubtedly have. Just being able to recognize that a day is awful is a type of progress because you are setting a standard for how you want to live and experience life.

You might not reach your dreams and that is okay.
Actually experiencing your biggest, wildest dream to its absolute end is not really what the road to success looks like. In reality, you most certainly will not have to wait that long for feelings of glee. What changes you, grows you, and makes you stronger is simply the process of working towards a massive achievement. If you achieve your biggest dream, then that undoubtedly will make you feel wonderful. However, making it to that great big finish line is not a requirement for enjoyment or for success. It is all the little stuff that drives you there that will make you happier, more empowered, and in time will completely transform you.

You do not have a direct relationship with the world.
Your understanding of reality comes via your senses of sight, sound, touch, smell, and taste. Together, they help you form an understanding of reality, your personal worldview. There are things that might get in the way of

you using your senses to get as accurate an understanding as is physically possible, but do not get frustrated if you disagree with others about the details. Just focus on maintaining as accurate of a worldview as you can, remembering that there is no such thing as perfect understanding.

There is an unlimited amount of good in the universe. You do not need to hurt someone else in order to feel happy or gain goodness. You can achieve your goals, have good things happen to you, or simply experience something positive without stealing it or taking from somewhere else. There is not some kind of hidden balance that must be maintained in order for reality to exist. It is okay to feel happy, take part in pleasing events and relationships, or otherwise experience joy.

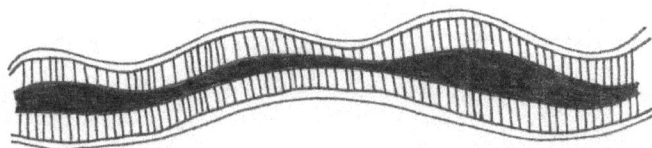

Allow your reactions to be short term. You may experience a great thing, but later feel disappointed in yourself for not holding on to the joy you felt for as long of a time as you wanted to. It is okay, and probably normal. Most emotional reactions do not span weeks and months. Allow the possibility that a bad event may cause a short-term negative reaction too. Free yourself from an expectation that if you achieve a certain goal then you will be elated for the rest of your life. It is also okay if you do not feel bad about something for your whole life. You have the right to free yourself from the burden of being a constant, lifelong suffer of a bad event or hardship. You do not have to carry negativity around with you forever just because an event will forever be bad. You reacted, so move onward and forward when you are ready.

Enjoy the decision making process. When you make a choice about how you are going to spend your time and energy, those small actions form the framework of your life. While making decisions may be stressful, you are capable of making it an enjoyable experience. Take a moment to be grateful for having some choice available and try your best to truly enjoy selecting your actions. Change can be a positive experience.

Happiness is a skill, not so much a talent. Sure, there are many factors that go into making you happy, but generally, it really is a skill. You can practice being happy by investing your energy and time into actions that are authentic and meaningful to you. Over time and by consistently committing to this on a personal level, your happiness will increase in your daily life.

Take actions to move forward with purpose. There are many decisions you can make that will move you forward in your life, but take the time to select the actions that you find meaningful. You ultimately decide what exactly is the most meaningful and which path fulfills your purpose. It might be scary to take actions that align with the purpose you find the most fulfilling, but it is through such authentic actions that you can expect the most rewards and success.

Consider the benefits of some stress. Having an expectation to eliminate all stress from your life might be counterproductive. Sometimes a little bit of stress is a good thing because it motivates you to take action and keep moving forward towards your dreams. If your job begins to create tension, it is your body's way of suggesting it is time to start applying for other jobs that inspire you. If your hobby starts to stress you out, then your body might be trying to communicate that you need different interests to keep growing. Allow yourself to view stress on small levels to be a tool to help you and not necessarily something you need to fight against, or always avoid.

Reexamine how you view your thoughts. At first glance, your thoughts might seem very abstract and ambiguous. Really take a hard look at them though, because thoughts are also things—tangible things. Try your best to collect and create good, positive ones. Over time, your collection will serve you well.

Focus more of your energy and thoughts on your process. Sometimes a job interview does not turn into a job offer. Sometimes a date will end horribly. Sometimes your good ideas at a meeting are not received well, or are not taken seriously. It is not a good feeling when your hard work does not immediately turn into the kind of outcome you want. Do your best not to take this personally. Adjust your expectations going into these situations. Instead of focusing your energy on getting results, shift your focus and energy to the process of your actions. Ask yourself what you learned from the process, or experience of your recent actions. You can ask yourself what you gained from the procedure of completing your most recent job interview. Ask yourself what valuable knowledge you learned from the process of preparing for, and going through with a date. Ask yourself how you presented your ideas at your recent meeting, and if there is anything you might do differently about the process you went through to prepare for that meeting. You cannot always control the results, so focusing on them might cause you to develop great frustrations, but you can control your actions, and how you process your reactions, so adjust your expectations accordingly to suit your long-term goals.

It is not a question of being a more perfect you, but rather just being more authentic. You might easily get sucked into an expectation that by behaving differently, you will be a better person and tend to view yourself as either doing an action perfectly or somehow imperfectly. Try to let go of this concept of perfect, and replace it with just the idea of the process of growth, and ask yourself if your actions are moving you forward in the direction you wish to go in your life. It is not about walking the perfect path, but walking the path you are on with authenticity.

Choose to anticipate success, rather than assume failure. There is no need to attach negativity to something that has not happened yet. However, taking a small amount of your energy to apply positivity to your envision of the future might provide you with more meaning today. Living in the present might seem more worthwhile if you can form a connection between your current actions and tomorrow's opportunities. Maybe working a summer job today might seem more worthwhile if you remind yourself, and anticipate how much joy you will get out of spending your hard-earned money next fall when you return to college. Maybe grocery shopping will feel much more enjoyable if you anticipate how delicious all of your home cooked meals will taste in the near future. Acknowledging the connection between the present and the future in a way that anticipates joy likely will motivate you.

Accept the current moment. Stop expecting the world to deliver your list of wants and needs upon command. The world does not work for you in this way. It is the provider of life and energy for every one and thing. Stop expecting it to favor you or your life. The world's role is neutral and in this powerful neutrality is exquisite beauty. Take a moment and appreciate the world. Stop and be thankful for its existence and for yours.

It takes hard, smart work to achieve goals. There is no avoiding work. Sure, you can work efficiently and there are smart ways to use your time, so that you are moving forward towards the kind of lifestyle you want for yourself. However, the path to success, no matter how you choose to define it will take some work on your part. Sometimes that work will be in the form of tasks that are not your favorite things to do. If you need to take a minimum wage job to open up a future opportunity, consider doing it. If you need to join a gym to get one-on-one help to exercise, consider restructuring your budget and schedule to make it happen. If you need to ask for tutoring help to pass a math class so you can work towards the education you desire, reach out for help. It is never beneath you to do hard stuff when they are the small stepping stones to building the kind of life you want to live, the future you want to experience.

V

Forming Realistic Relationships with Others

It is one thing to form a better understanding of what drives and empowers you, but it is another task to form healthy relationships with other people. Not every person is on the same path in life as you. Therefore, it is not easy to relate to everyone all of the time.

In this final section, you will find many pieces of advice and wisdom for interacting with others. Many may feel more like reminders than insights, but sometimes reading something written in a short and simple way may provide a lot of clarity. Keep in mind that sometimes it is the little acts of love that make all the difference. Small actions may bring a great deal of happiness and goodness into your life's relationships.

◇◇◇◇◇◇◇◇

It is always okay to ask for help. You may have to ask several different people before you get the help you are looking for, but keep asking. Not everyone can provide you with the kind of help you are looking for, so do not feel bad if you have to keep searching for assistance. You may even need to ask the same person more than once and that too is okay.

Do not obsessively worry about how people react to you. The people in your life are responsible for their own health and wellbeing, not you. If people you know seem to pull away, let them. They may need a little bit more space to recharge and process how best to help you with your current hardship. Some may pull away completely. Let them. What you are experiencing might be difficult for those who love you to watch, and some may be too weak to stay by your side. Forgive them and let them go. Allow room for others to enter into your life.

Make healthy connections with others. Part of forming new relationships is simply reaching out to form new connections. Interacting with others comes in a variety of forms. You can met an acquaintance for coffee, form a new hiking club in your area, or write a response to an online post or blog that was meaningful to you. Take the time to form connections that provide you with energy and uplift your spirits. Surround yourself with positive connections, ones that inspire you to grow and are based on experiences that promote joy.

Get in the habit of saying thank you. It may take a long time and lots of work to get what you need. By the time you receive it, you may seem exhausted and bitter because it took so long to get something you desperately needed, but tell the person you are thankful for their help anyway. It is the first step towards forming a positive relationship with the person. It may be a small act, but it solidifies your commitment to forming more relationships that are positive in your life.

Accept feedback, but do not always take it personally. This is easier said than done, but you need to try your best to listen to feedback. The feedback that people give you may be useful, but often only to a degree. Unfortunately, it does not take much for the feedback you receive to take on a life of its own and begin to become a put down. Sometimes feedback can be extremely hurtful, if you let it. Focus on the useful bits and mentally trash the rest. Occasionally, a person that communicates with you may just lack tact. That is a reflection of their communication skills, not your worth.

You will probably receive some bad advice. Not everyone will, or can be supportive. Sometimes a person will attempt to offer advice or help that frankly is more hurtful than helpful. You probably are not interested in listening to someone provide you with the quickest route to the post office via car when you are traveling via bicycle. You probably do not want to listen to someone explain how to make the best meatloaf when you are a vegetarian. People mean well, okay, *usually* they mean well. You are going through something that most cannot imagine—your own unique life. It is to be expected that sometimes their best intentions fall short. Do not expect every piece of advice you hear to be good for you.

Do not expect anyone or anything to swoop in and fix your life. There is no magic pill that you take just once and instantly you feel better. There is no specialist that is so talented that after one visit with him or her, you will feel well. It took time for current situation, your current life to develop and it will take time for your actions to create a more positive life for yourself. Try your best to be patient. It often takes time for meaningful changes to fully transform your life. Sure, occasionally, you will experience a great, moving moment that will motivate you forward. However, in the long run, it is your work and determination that will bring you to where you want to be.

We are all connected and we all impact each other. Often we do not realize this or even understand how exactly we do so. When you are having a good day and smile at strangers, it influences them. If you are having a bad day, and take it out on others, this also affects them. While it is not your responsibility to make everyone around you feel good, it is your responsibility to treat others with respect. If you are experiencing a negative mood, then now might not be the best time to run errands. Wait an hour, have a snack, or go for a walk first. Acknowledge that you share this world with others and attempt to make positive connections, even with strangers.

Forgive a stranger. You may find that your life path intersections with people who happen to be jerks, rude, or otherwise just plain mean. It is hard to let go immediately after someone cuts you off in traffic, or when someone rudely talks loud on their cell phone, or when someone buys the last strawberry banana muffin you have been looking forward to purchasing since you arose from you bed this morning. It is difficult, but instead of allowing their actions to create further stress in your life, you can forgive them. After all, they are strangers and since you will not ever see them again prevent yourself from seeing their negativity again by letting it go.

Others may not seek change. That is not your burden to carry. Throughout the process of transforming yourself and your life, you may realize that there are people in your life with unhealthy habits. You cannot make another person seek help or expect them be receptive to confrontations to change. If the relationship you have with someone is unhealthy or negatively influencing your ability to live a positive life, you may need to let go of that relationship. You may need to open your heart and mind to modifying the relationship or letting other, healthier people into your life.

It is not your place to judge others. You may know that someone could do more. You may disagree with a decision they have made. You may believe that their actions are bad, or even morally wrong. It is not your job to pass judgment on them. Just as you have the right to decide how you spend your time, other people do too. You may passionately disagree with someone's decision, but it is possible to respect his or her decision without passing judgment.

You do not have to explaining everything. When you are dealing with hardship, you did not also become the voice box for this particular problem. It is not your job to discuss, describe, and explain what it is or is not. Your number one job right now is to take care of you, which might take a lot of your time and energy. Spend your energy on you and do not worry about educating other people about the hardships of the world. There are many individuals working on such problems for you so that you do not have to. Right now, just focus on you.

Choose to be picky about who you call your friend.
There are billions of people in the world and many of them speak the same language you do. You can set high standards for which people you let into your life. Keep in mind that you can have different kinds of relationships in your life. Some people might make great acquaintances, but not very good friends. It is okay to admit you like listening to your eccentric neighbor's stories about hiking through desert canyons but not want to invite her over for tea. You really do not have to let perfectly nice couple join your game night just because they ask, especially if they seem always to reek of eye watering, throat gagging perfume. Other people may seem like amazing people, but not the kind that you need in your life right now. It is okay to say no, to set boundaries and have standards. Just remember to be kind and nice about it, or think of alternative social situations that are more appropriate and make you feel more comfortable.

You do not have to do everything that people advise you to do. Every so often, the advice you get is horrible. People may feel that since they know what to do to feel better, then they are now the expert on what makes everyone happy. Their logic is that since you both are

141

human, then as a fellow human it must work for you too. It is faulty logic. Generally, people mean the best for you, but their ideas are not always practical. Simply extend your thanks and keep doing what you need to do to increase your happiness.

Do not assume you know what other people are thinking and feeling. You are unique and so is every other human on the planet. Every person experiences life in his or her own way. It is not appropriate to assume you can guess what someone is thinking or feeling. Their behavior or body language might provide clues, but instead of assuming, try asking. If he or she does not wish to share, do not pressure them. You can respect another person's privacy. You probably would want the same respect shown to you.

Respect other people's space. Every person has a right to private space, both physically and mentally. Each person may need or desire a different amount of privacy. Allow people to choose what amount of privacy they want. Do your best to respect their decision. It may be hard, but put forth the effort to let others set their own boundaries. It will help you form positive relationships with the people in your life.

You may find that your significant other cannot provide all the support you need. In most relationships, he or she cannot, which is why it is healthy to have friends, and other types of people in your life. It does not mean you are needy or hard to handle. It means you are normal. It is okay to look outside of your closest relationships for extra support. You are not doing anything wrong if you want to make new friends, join a club, or get a second opinion. Just keep in mind what is appropriate for each type of relationship and strive to not to cross any boundaries.

Attempt to identify what kind of support you need. Then ask for it. You might know exactly what you need in order to solve a problem by yourself. It is okay to ask for resources, support, and tools. Some might be more open to helping you solve a problem when you provide specific requests.

It is not your responsibility to make everyone around you happy. You may gain something from pleasing other people. It may be easier to please others than yourself, but it is not your responsibility to do so. You do not need to base your decisions on what will make others happy. You are allowed to make yourself happy. It is okay and a fun part of life.

Speak up when you need something. Your needs may seem obvious to you, but they are usually not obvious to others. You will need to advocate for yourself when you need help. You likely will have to do this every time you need something. It requires a lot of energy and it may be very hard, but you can do it. You can speak up for yourself. Each time you do, it gets easier.

Two different opinions can both be right. Some scenarios or topics have no wrong answer, which means everyone is right. You can disagree with another and that does not mean that you are a lesser person or wrong in any way. It just means you have an equally valid, but different opinion.

There are more options than just winning and losing. Many people enter into a conversation or argument with the idea that there are only two outcomes: to win or to loose. This is a very unhealthy way to view human interaction. There are many other outcomes. It is possible to enter into a discussion and for everyone to leave with all that he or she needs. Focus on identifying what you need, how to accurately communicate that need, and be open to meeting your need without fighting for it. Occasionally, just asking is all that is required to get your needs met.

There is probably more you can do in your relationships. Before assuming that other parties are to blame in your relationships, take a hard look at your actions. There may be more you can do. Do not trivialize the small stuff. The only person you can control in any relationship is you. If you can do more, then do so. If you cannot, then perhaps you need to change the relationship, alter how you perceive the connection between you and the other person, or leave it. You only have a limited amount of energy to extend, so choose to use it in the most positive, most beneficial way for you.

It is okay to be ungrateful. You do not have to love the present you received. You do not have to find the help given useful. It is fine if you really are not appreciative of what some else does for you. You really do not have to force yourself to like what your spouse buys you on your birthday. You really do not have to enjoy eating the pancakes your children tried to make you, especially if their base ingredient was soy sauce. Always give the benefit of the doubt, give gifts a chance. The advice or present received might really work for you once you give it an opportunity to work. Regardless, it is most certainly a good idea to still thank the person for their time, their hard work, or their effort, but you by no means owe anyone your full gratitude.

Give the people in your life a break. If someone is unable to provide the support you need, be forgiving. If someone has provided advice based on bad information, be compassionate. You may desire a kind of support they are not capable of giving. A person can love you and care about you, but just not be able to provide the kind of support you desire right now. That is okay. Try to accept people as they are and forgive.

Some things may need to stay a private matter. Stop and consider how it is best to express what you are going through. Maybe writing in a journal is best. Maybe keeping some things between you and one other trusted individual is best. While it is okay to get it out in the open, you probably need to be selective about how you do it. It is okay if someone does not want to hear about an aspect of your life. You probably have lived days that even you find boring, so refrain from setting abnormally high expectations for others. They have the right not to listen just as you have the right to want to speak. You can process your thoughts privately. You have that power and ability to do so.

Consider joining a group or taking a class. An excellent way to meet people is to try new activities. One way to make a go at new things is to join an organization, club, or take a class. Research what is available in your area. There often are inexpensive offerings through city or state sponsored programs. Ask for help if you struggle to find something that might interest you. There are also many classes online, some are free. Taking a class online may potentially be helpful, but sometimes classes where you meet people in person are better. It often is easier to meet new people and talk to them when you can see them face to face.

Rejections are just missed opportunities. You may provide someone with an opportunity and he or she chooses not to take advantage of it. You may feel rejected, but in reality, you were not rejected. Instead, your opportunity was rejected. Others have the right to not take advantage of your opportunities, just as you have the right to say no too. Someone may not want to be your friend, your date, or your partner in crime. That is okay, let others be. You are not a person of lesser worth because your offer was not accepted.

Choose to be your own cheerleader. Give yourself compliments when you need them. It is not weird, it is a smart way to practice positive self-talk. When you expect others to give you the compliments you crave, you are waiting for someone else's permission to enjoy your life. Do not wait on others to bring joy into your day. You have the power to praise yourself.

Fight issues and problems, not people. When discussing a conflict, or if you find yourself in the middle of an argument, focus on the issue at hand. Try to avoid bringing up past emotions or arguments. Resist the urge to engage in name-calling. There might be a part of you that really wants to call another human on the planet a scumbag, prick, or politely explain that the leftovers growing mold in your refrigerator currently process more intelligence than him or her. Rise above the temptation. Focus on the current discussion, and devote effort to simply resolving the issue at the heart of the matter.

Minimize comparing yourself and your life to others. It is okay to observe another person or their life for a few moments, but do not determine your life's value based on that comparison. It is by taking action, living your own life, and determining your self-worth independently of any outside event that you will most likely experience the healthiest life in your power to create.

Make sure you are showing up to social commitments. It is one thing to appear physically at an event, but another to appear mentally and emotionally as well. Do your best to be fully present in all of your relationships with others, even the casual one-time interactions with strangers. It likely will help you feel more connected and in time, you will find these interactions more fulfilling.

Try to connect with others over positive shared circumstances. You may meet new people who share in your pain and sorrows, but also attempt to connect with people who share your dreams or aspirations. Surrounding yourself with relationships formed out of positive connections may help you progress towards the kind of optimistic future you are building for yourself. It can create an overall more healthy social life.

It is okay to say no. You may pass on opportunities when you need to. If a commitment would drain you of your energy, it might be best to pass on the chance for the experience. It is a big world with lots of opportunities for you. It is okay to let a few pass by because they are not a good fit for you right now.

Stay away from and out of gossip. You may go to the source of the story or simply ignore it if you wish to find peace faster. Repeating stories based on hearsay or talking about people while they are not present may add stress to your life. You are devoting energy and focus to something that probably will not improve your overall state of health.

Make an effort to remain silent if gossip comes up in conversation. In time, the topic will change and you can contribute again.

Take care of yourself first. It may be hard to put yourself first, but you likely will feel less stressed if you make your wellbeing a priority. There is no need to self-indulge, but by investing a little more energy into your own health, you will have more energy to devote to the wellbeing of those around you. In a big way, helping yourself will often help others.

Do not waste your energy on fighting history. Allow the past to remain in the past. Resist the temptation to bring up past emotions and conflict into current arguments or conversations. Focus your energy and time on the present. Allow yourself the freedom to only be responsible for this current moment in time.

Set out to meet new people. It is okay to take up a hobby or attend events with the intent to meet new people. Just remember that it takes time to develop a friendship, so start small. Greet people and invest the energy to engage in small talk.

Refrain from thinking about what to say next. When in conversation, try not to think ahead by rehearsing in your mind what you want to say. Instead, focus on the person you are speaking with and give him your full attention. Giving your undivided attention is a simple way to express commitment to the situation. Doing so will often help you listen better, which is always a good skill to develop further. This practice will likely help you create healthier relationships.

You do not need to connect every conversation back to you. It is okay just to listen when someone is speaking without interjecting a story about your own life that is similar. It is okay to just let someone tell a very long story about how she was stuck in airport security when flying home for the holidays, as if she was the only person in the history of people to have experienced this. It really is okay to let someone, for a few minutes, be the star of her life story and of the conversation. It is not necessary to identify with every individual you encounter either. It is okay to have social interactions where you allow a person to tell you his whole story so you can truly get to know her and hear what she has to say. You might know nothing about hiking boots, but find yourself listening to a very complex and complicated rendition of how to most efficiently research hiking gear. It is okay, just listen and try to learn more about the other person. Showing this simple act of patience and compassion does lots of good for everyone involved.

Practice paraphrasing. A great life skill to develop is paraphrasing or summarizing. You state in your own words what was just stated in conversation. It allows you to you communicate that you are actually listening and gives you the opportunity to make sure that you are getting all the information accurately. You are never too old to mindfully be more aware of how you well you are listening. You may accidently mishear something or get distracted. Paraphrasing allows you to check into the social interaction in a way that does not require you to open up, which may sometimes feel safer and cause less anxiety.

It is okay if you do not like someone. You do not have to love every single person you meet. There are billions of people on the planet. Odds are you might not like some of them. That is fine. What is not okay is disrespecting people or allowing your dislike to grow into hate. Give yourself permission to admit you might not like everyone, knowing that you can continue to be kind and compassionate to all.

Watch your tone when speaking. You communicate a lot with the volume and type of pitch of your voice. A whisper communicates meaning and so does shouting. Even if you spoke the exact same words, each level of tone adds more meaning to what you are trying to say. Be mindful of everything you are expressing when you speak.

Commit to resolving conflict in a positive way. There are healthy ways to deal with conflict. It is not about always being on top, but rather how to handle the stress, and create solutions that will improve the lives of all involved. Focus more on prioritizing the issues at hand and resolving one conflict at a time. Stay in the present moment. There is no need to bring up old disagreements or drag more than one problem into the discussion. You deserve to improve your life through conflict resolution in a manner that does not give you more stress or hardship.

You can ask that others let go of details. Many times in a conversation, you may be expected to provide specific information. One easy thing to ask from others is to request they help by giving you some slack on providing those details, especially while coping with any kind of hardship or difficulty. While working through a tough personal situation, making an effort to recount such details is probably difficult and to be asked to so may only create additional stress and unnecessary negativity. Listen to your intuition, speak up when you need to, but allow yourself the ability to focus on what is positive for you right now, in this moment. You may need to share your story, or you may not. That is fine. Just remember you do not owe anyone a detailed account of the past events of your life. You write your own life story. You decide which details are meaningful. You choose when and how to share them, if ever.

You can say no. Practice saying no more often when you are asked to do something you do not feel comfortable doing, or would otherwise rob you of your energy. You deserve to use your energy to propel your life forward towards a healthier future. It is okay to say no.

You probably will not receive praise from others and that is okay. You do not need to wait around for other people in your life to give you credit for a job well done. You know when you are giving it your all and when things go well. Choose to give yourself praise when you deserve it and as often as you want.

Refrain from dumping your feelings onto others. You do not have the right to bundle up your negative emotions and throw them at other humans. Instead, find healthier channels to release negative energy. Try taking a walk, building something, listening to music, or practicing calming breathing exercises. You do have control over when you choose to work all of that negativity out of your body, so choose to stay kind to others.

Give compliments often. Say nice things to others and to yourself. Praise things and decisions you like or find enjoyable. If you admire your friend's choice in shoes, say so. If you are impressed with your neighbor's garden, tell him. You do not need to wait for an invitation to share your admiration.

Finding new friends is about finding new places. If you continue with the same routines, you will keep running into the same people. Check out an events calendar, research other areas in your community, and seek out activities that interest you. At first, you might be going alone, but in time, you will meet new people. Some may eventually become your friends. If you continue with the same routines and frequent the same places, it might be difficult to encounter new, healthier people to bring into your life when you want to make room for new relationships.

Give an hour of your time. Your time is a gift. Choose to dedicate an hour of it to another person. Help a neighbor mow her lawn, listen to a family member tell a story, assist a friend with a move, or spend an hour volunteering in your community. You most likely will find some sense of purpose in helping others and it may help take your thoughts off your struggles for a short while.

There may be people you encounter who just will never understand. Stop wasting your time and energy explaining things to them. It is not your duty to drag others out of their ignorance. You may find it useful to share resources with them, but stop short of taking on the responsibility of their enlightenment. That is their journey in their life and certainly not your top priority right now. Redirect all of that energy and passion towards your own life and goals.

Take ownership of your actions. You may need or want to do something, which is fine. Call your actions what they are, your actions. They are a reflection of your needs and your wants, no one else's. You are under no obligation to do things for others. If you do, it is because you wanted to, so accept that. Take ownership of your choice of actions.

You can disagree with an idea without disliking its creator. Sometimes you may really dislike a thought, opinion, or idea and that is okay. You can say so. You can tell your friend, doctor, loved one, or stranger that their idea is not great and still believe the person is a good person. Try not to intertwine a person's worth with their actions. Sometimes a wonderful person will have a lapse in judgment and say something really offense or illogical. Every person has value that is independent of his or her behavior, including you. Try your best to practice compassion and be understanding when these minor slip-ups happen.

You are equal to all others. You are not more important than any other person, nor are you any less important. On some basic level, you are of equal worth to your worst enemy and your greatest hero. It may be a challenging idea to accept, but accepting this truth will really decrease a lot of negativity that you may be holding onto in your life. A practicing Christian is not a better person, on this basic human level, than a practicing Muslim or even an atheist. An American of European descent is not a better person, on this basic human level, as someone who is of African or Asian descent. A college graduate is not a better person, on this basic human level, than a high school dropout. You may have different experiences and beliefs, but you are still equally important as any other living human in the general grand scheme of human life that occupies this planet and universe. It is through an understanding of basic

157

sameness, this human connection, that compassion can develop and continuous respect can take place. It is within your power to be kind, on a basic human level, to everyone you encounter, even when it is hard, even when you really dislike how the other person lives their life, and especially when you really do not feel like it. Be kind and respectful always, even when it hurts.

Accept that there exists diversity among people in the area of spiritual and philosophical ideals. You have the ability to choose from among a wide variety of existing ideas, belief systems, and philosophies. Whatever area of thought or faith you select is often fine as long as it serves you well. Remember that others have the same freedom you do. Try to refrain from assumptions and judgments. Others may use their own beliefs to justify passing judgment on you, but you do not need to stoop to their level of spite.

Your needs are valid, but so are the needs of others. When you find yourself in an argument, remember that your needs are not the only important ones. Strive to find solutions to disagreements that meet the needs of all those involved in the conflict. A good resolution will ensure that the needs of everyone are met effectively.

Some people are just bad for you and that is really okay. You may encounter perfectly nice people that are unhealthy for you. You might cross paths with someone who seems always to choose to behave unkindly towards you. There are many reasons why a person is just not good for you. All those reasons are okay reasons for not letting him or her close to you. You deserve to have both healthy relationships and people who are good for you in your life.

People tend to remember how you make them feel. When you encounter other people attempt to finish your conversation with something positive like a saying you are thankful for their time or shaking their hand good-bye. A simple phrase of spoken gratitude might result in recharging or uplifting the other person in the conversation, and he or she most likely will remember feeling that goodness when around you. Provoking positive feelings of warmth and kindness can go a long way to establishing trusting and healthy relationships.

Set healthy boundaries between yourself and others. You have the ability and power to set standards for how you are treated in all of your relationships. You can also choose to enforce them by restating your expectations and removing yourself from any situation that makes you feel unsafe. You deserve to spend your time with people who are healthy for you.

Not all can love you the way you need to be loved. It is okay if you reach out for emotional support and the person you want to help you simply cannot. You do not have control over what a person is capable of providing. A person may love you very much and will show his or her love any way he or she can, but not in every single way you need. You have not done anything wrong, nor has the person you reached out to for assistance. Accept that there are some kinds of love only you can provide for yourself. It is ultimately your responsibility to fill this need. Practice showing yourself kindness and compassion.

There is little need to attract a large audience. You may wish to reach out for support, which is fine, but try to draw a line. Make sure you do not share so much that you violate healthy boundaries. Not every little thing needs to be shared with a wide audience online via a blog or video. Frankly, there are probably some experiences that in hindsight are rather silly and while you enjoyed them at the moment, you do not wish to relive them. Dressing up with your roommates like pirates and walking through downtown at midnight was probably a lot of fun, but also something you do not want to share on the internet to relive later when you are in negotiations with a well-respected company for a lucrative position. You may have enjoyed sampling every brand of jelly from your local grocery store, but there is no need to broadcast a photo of your daily slice of jelly covered toast on a blog. There is such a thing as excessive sharing. Part of the process of change and growth involves practicing self-validation, which is difficult if you share too much information with others. Start to keep a private journal to begin the work of validating parts of your life. Live more in the moment and value experiences as they come, or just keep some things to yourself for your own private enjoyment. Sharing is good, but you can keep it healthy.

Others do not have to cooperate. You may have a fantastic plan. You may have thought about it forwards and backwards. You may know that it has no flaws at all and yet you might still encounter someone who refuses to cooperate. It happens. Everyone, including you, has the right to not go along with an idea or plan. Try not to waste your time hoping for people to change, just make small changes to your plan or change your expectations.

Stick to specifics when you ask for things you want. Even if you speak up and request something, without giving details, it might still be hard to receive what you want. Making a general statement about how you would like to go out more, spend more time alone, or get more attention probably will not result in getting what you actually want. Try stating details like on what days you wish to go out and where you want to visit. Try explaining how you define being alone as just being in a room by yourself or maybe you really do want the whole house to be free of company. Consider stating that you want eye contact from a family member when you speak or perhaps the kind of attention you seek is just the opportunity to spend more time with others. Being direct most likely will result in more success.

Choose to be aware of nonverbal communication.
When you are having a conversation, keep in mind how your tone of voice, body language, and facial expressions might alter the meaning of the words you are speaking. It is okay if you accidently communicate more than you mean to when speaking with others. Just be more mindful of nonverbal behavior and continue practicing your best communication skills. You are never too old to further develop your understanding of how to most effectively communicate with others. It is not something that is learned once during toddlerhood, and then you no longer need to expand on this skill. It is something you can continue to cultivate over your lifetime.

Conflict and frustration are normal parts of relationships. Disagreements are common and typical. You are not a bad person just because you encounter conflict in one of your relationships. The important aspect to focus on is how you behave and react to the conflict. No matter how you feel about a person or situation, you can still treat all involved, including yourself, with respect. Yes, it is true that pelting others with water balloons or investing in a bullhorn might be more entertaining, but it is not healthy. Choose to be healthy and respectful. Choose to be caring and mature, even when faced with frustration.

Refrain from trying to place blame. For many things in life, there just is simply no one at fault. If you obsess over trying to find someone or something to blame, you miss out on simply living your life to the fullest extent possible. There is a huge difference between accepting blame and taking responsibility. Focus more on owning your responsibility. You can use it to empower yourself by taking control and making changes to better suit your needs.

Harming others for your benefit or amusement is never appropriate. There are many ways to achieve your goals. Choose a path that does not involve hurting anyone. This also includes you. It is possible with practice to live a healthier life. There is no need to resort to being anything less than a kind, compassionate person when working on creating a better future for you.

Respect is most commonly something that is earned. It is within your power to extend respect to everyone you encounter, but refrain from assuming you will instantly have the respect of others in return. It is through your actions of demonstrated responsibility that you will probably earn the respect of most people you meet. It is impossible to literally earn the respect of everyone. This is simply because you cannot foresee how individuals are going to execute their right to free thinking and frankly, you probably do not want to intrude on another's freedom anyway. Accept that occasionally you may encounter a person, for probably a reason that you will ever understand, will choose to not find you worthy of their respect. Let such people be, and try to make room in your heart and life for people who are healthier and better for you. You want people in your life to acknowledge your demonstrated actions of responsibility and extend to you reasonable amounts of earned recognition and respect. You have the power to allow only these kinds of healthy relationships dominate your life.

There is an unlimited amount of goodness, even in social situations. There is no need to bring someone down in order to be powerful or worthy of love and happiness. Your self-worth and value does not depend on the well-being of other people, or the lack of others being successful and happy. You have not failed at life just because your friend got a promotion and you did not. You have not failed at any of your roles or any aspect of your identity just because a co-worker got a raise or because your neighbors purchased a new car. It is not a competition, but a journey. You are on your own journey, and therefore continue to love yourself unconditionally and focus on the process and actions you need to in order to move forward towards the future you want to live.

Strive for more interactions that are actually in person. It is easy to connect with people over the internet, through social media sites. There is much socialization and many intellectual exchanges you can enjoy from such interactions. However, you will probably gain more and have much more healthy relationships if you can connect with your friends over shared experiences in the real world. Go for a jog with a friend, invite an acquaintance to the movies, and build on the connections you make by adding more shared, real world experiences to your history together.

Give others the benefit of the doubt. Refrain from being quick to assume that your current inconvenience was personal and deliberate. A long line at the grocery store might be due to a cashier calling in sick, leaving one cashier to do the work of two. An item might be out of stock because the store manager found the item shipped to be of low quality and sent it back. A package might be delayed because of unforeseen bad weather. You can waste a lot of energy being disappointed and angry about things not going your way, but try not to assume that it is personal. It takes a lot of effort to get upset and irritated standing in a long line, checking in again with a store later, or waiting an extra day for a package. Odds are that no one planned to make you wait at the store, or make you take two trips, or meant for you to not have your mail on time. Sure, others may set high expectations, even money back guarantees, but just as no one is perfect, no system is perfect either. Choose to assume good, choose to be flexible, and choose to be kind.

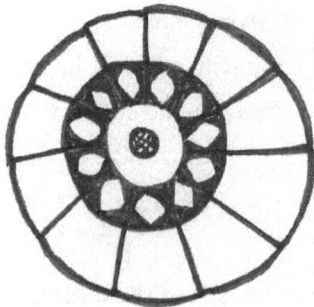

Dear Reader,

I hope that you have found the *Jolly Doodle Edition* of *Tidbits of Insight for Creating Optimism* to be a worthy read. I really enjoyed writing this book because I believe in its positive message.

When I wrote my first book, *500 Tidbits of Insight: Living with and Overcoming Depression*, I realized that I had failed to connect with some of my readers because of how the content was formatted. This book's development originated out of a desire to connect to those readers and reach out to a wider audience on the more general topic of optimism and creating personal happiness.

Artwork was included to add to the overall mood and provide a little bit of entertainment. Doing so has created an odd beast of a book and perhaps an unusual reading experience. I am a firm believer in experimenting with new concepts. It is my hope that the combination of short thoughtful tidbits alongside some simple drawings was a good experience and one that you felt was worthy of your time.

If you wish to purchase your own copy of any of the Jolly Doodles, just visit my website at www.TidbitsOfInsight.com. There you will find a variety product for purchase. You will even find lots of designs that did not make the cut for this book, but look great on coffee mugs, t-shirts, and other fun stuff.

I would love to hear from you! You can write me at malonebooks@gmail.com or visit my website at www.TidbitsOfInsight.com. I also ask that you please review my book because it is feedback from readers that help me understand what is truly useful and insightful. Consider posting this feedback publicly, the good and the bad, on a website like Amazon or Goodreads so that your powerful words can connect with other readers and inspire others to voice their opinions too.

Thank you for taking the time to read my book,

K. DeLaughter.

Reading Group Questions

1. Did you feel that this book fulfilled your expectations? Why or why not?

2. Did you enjoy the author's choice of format? Did this writing style help you relate to the tidbits more easily than other books you have read in this genre or on similar topics?

3. What would you say is the central idea discussed in the book? Do you think that K. DeLaughter does a thorough job of providing sufficient insight on the topic?

4. Do you believe the issues discussed in the book affect your life directly? How so?

5. How much of your overall happiness or optimism do you believe is built from within and is within your control?

6. What limitations or obstacles get in your way and prevent you from achieving your optimal amount of optimism? What causes these limitations or obstacles?

7. Do you find the ideas and perspectives presented by the author practical? Are the solutions proposed realistic?

8. After providing ideas about how to build optimism on an individual basis, the author spends her final chapter talking about methods of maintaining that optimism while interacting with others. Do you think this chapter was helpful? Why or why not?

9. What have you learned from this book? Has it helped you discover anything new about yourself?

10. Which tidbits did you find the most valuable or useful for your life?

Suggested Readings

Allison, Jay & Dan Gediman (Eds.). (2006). *This I believe: The personal philosophies of remarkable men and women.* New York, NY: Henry Holt and Company.

Dalai Lama and Victor Chan. (2004). *The wisdom of forgiveness: Intimate conversations and journeys.* New York, NY: Riverhead Books.

Ehrenreich, Barbara. (2009). *Bright-sided: How the relentless promotion of positive thinking has undermined America.* New York, NY: Henry Holt and Company.

Ellis, Neenah. (2004). *If I Live to be 100: Lessons from the centenarians.* New York, NY: Three Rivers Press. (Original work published 2002)

Frankl, Viktor E. (2006). *Man's search for meaning.* Boston, MA: Beacon Press. (Original work published 1946)

Gladwell, Malcom. (2007). *Blink: The power of thinking without thinking.* New York, NY: Back Bay Books. (Original work published 2005)

Press, Eyal. (2012). *Beautiful souls: Saying no, breaking ranks, and heeding the voice of conscience in dark times.* New York, NY: Farrar, Straus, and Giroux.

Rubin, Gretchen. (2009). *The happiness project: Or, why I spent a year trying to sing in the morning, clean my closets, fight right, read Aristotle, and generally have more fun.* New York, NY: HarperCollins Publishers.

Weiner, Eric. (2008). *The geography of bliss: One grump's search for the happiest places in the world.* New York, NY: Twelve.

Zander, Rosamund Stone & Benjamin Zander. (2002). *The art of possibility.* New York, NY: Penguin Books. (Original work published 2000)

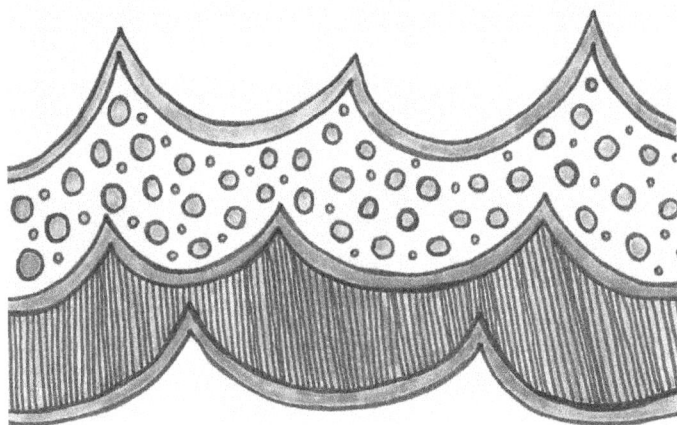